A DETERMINED BLACK LAB

by

Thomas Kendrick

ISBN: 9781734905502 (paperback)

Cover design: Write Plan

Copyeditor and proofreader: Stephanie Cham

Formatting and Ebook: ebookpbook.com

Rex was a good friend.
—Thomas Kendrick.

TABLE OF CONTENTS

CAT FOOD

"It's hard to beat a black Lab."

That was the sales pitch Tom tried to ignore as he sat and worked at his desk that afternoon. Fred rolled his chair closer as he described the eight mixed Lab puppies, he was so eager to part ways with.

This conversation was taking place because his full-blooded female Labrador had joined up with a male mutt roaming around the neighborhood.

"That floozy," an eavesdropping coworker added. Neither amused nor discouraged, Fred continued to pitch the idea of Tom coming by that afternoon and picking out one of the puppies to take home.

"Hot damn!" Tom yelled. Shocked for a half-second, Fred leaned back in his chair. "Dude, if you don't want to be bothered with those puppies today, that's cool, but be calm about it."

Both guys were dispatchers with a trucking company in Oakville, and Tom was trying to find an available driver to cover a load that one of his guys was broken down under.

"I just found a driver, and he belongs to you."

"Oh yeah, who is it?" asked Fred.

"Roscoe Tate. Looks like he's on vacation about ten miles away from where my guy is in the shop."

"I think the key word there is 'vacation'; he's off until Monday," Fred answered.

Tom stood, dropped his pen on the desk, and continued a sales pitch of his own. "No problem. The delivery is in Mobile, and we have until noon Monday to make it. Roscoe is only a couple hours away from Mobile; he can sleep late Monday morning and still be there on time."

"He will like that," Fred thought aloud.

"I'll have my guy haul the load to Roscoe's house, where it should be secure, then send him back to the shop," Tom added. He sat back in his chair, proud of himself for solving his last problem of the day.

"Fine with me; call Roscoe and let him know the plan. I'm headed home. I've done enough damage for the day. You're still dropping by to look at those dogs, right?" Fred asked.

"Yeah, I should be there in about twenty minutes."

While driving, Tom still wasn't sold on the idea of taking one of those puppies, but he was sure that getting Fred off his back about it was a good idea, and he felt the only way that would happen was if he went by and acted like he was interested.

Pulling into Fred's yard, he could hear two dogs barking while following him up the driveway. One was Marcy, a three-year-old, female, full-blooded black Lab and the mother of the puppies; the other was Emma, a large, female German shepherd that Fred had owned for years.

"Gosh, I forgot Emma was still alive," Tom said as he got out of the car.

"Oh yeah, she's a gentle giant." Fred stepped off the front porch.

Emma was pushing eleven years old, and it looked like she was carrying all those years on her back as she gingerly walked up to greet Tom.

"Hey, pretty girl, are you moving around slow today?"

"It's arthritis; I give her two pills a day for it. It's sad, really. Five years ago there wasn't an animal on this farm tame or wild that could outrun her, outplay her or outfight her. I guess if we all live long enough, Father Time has the last laugh. Okay, let's head to the dog pen, the wife will be home in about an hour, and I promised to have supper on the table when she gets here."

"You know, I should sit you down one day and explain what's causing all these puppies," Tom joked as he rubbed Emma's head.

The dog pen was a twenty-by-thirty fenced-in space equipped with a doghouse, doggy swimming pool, and shade from a hundred-year-old oak tree.

"Nice pen," observed Tom.

On weekdays, Marcy and Emma stayed inside the fence, which also served as a doggy daycare whenever puppies were on the property.

Fred whistled a couple of times and patted his leg to let the pups know they had a guest. Two little black heads appeared from the doghouse as if they were playing peekaboo. Once they recognized who it was, the two small pups came running, wagging their short tails so hard they almost wiggled themselves to the ground. Then another black one came trotting from behind the pool. Two more brown pups came running from behind the doghouse.

"Okay, that's five. Where are the other three?" asked Tom.

Fred stood on his tiptoes and looked over the fence, as if that would change the view. "I guess the others are asleep."

As he opened the door to the pen, puppy barks and puppy growls could be heard coming from inside the doghouse. "Sounds like there's a bad dog in there," Tom said.

As if on cue, three pups came rolling out of the little house, wrestling with each other and biting each other's tails and paws. All three were covered in dirt and sand, but none of them seemed bothered by it.

"Look at those little rascals go. Now that's entertainment," Fred bragged.

As Tom stood there, he was wondering to himself about the father. He was no dog expert, but the black puppies looked full-blooded Lab to him.

"So, what's the story on the father of these pups?"

"Don't know," Fred said. "Like I was saying at work, this litter was an accident. I never saw the father. Why?"

Tom bent down and picked up one of the black pups, examining it from head to toe. It was a female and didn't appreciate being lifted off the ground. "I think this litter has two fathers, and one was a full-blooded Lab or at least very close to it. See how the black ones are solid black, the other pups are different shades of brown and seem to be larger," Tom explained. He eased the puppy back onto the ground.

As Fred bent down to break up the wrestling match still happening on top of his boots between the three pups, he noticed something for the first time. "Well, I can't believe it," he said.

"What?" Tom asked.

"This black one."

"What about him?"

"He's bobtailed, the little mean ass has a nub where his tail should be. Maybe that brown one he was fighting with bit it off just now." Tom took a step toward the black puppy.

As they looked the little male pup over, they both decided that his lack of a tail was not an injury but something he'd been born with.

"Okay, you still think the black ones are full-blooded Lab? How many bobtailed Labs have you ever seen?" asked Fred.

Tom reached for the small fellow and pulled him in for a closer look. "I do believe this is the first one," he answered with a grin.

Fred rolled his eyes and shook his head. "Well, he may be missing a tail, but the way he was slinging those other two puppies around tells me he has plenty of heart," he said.

"Hey, little man, what happened to your tail?" While being held, the puppy had become calm as he looked straight into Tom's eyes, then begun to hassle.

"He's showing off his pretty white puppy teeth," Fred observed. "Looks like he's laughing."

"You were giving those other two puppies trouble. They had it coming, didn't they?" Tom asked his new friend.

The pup was solid black except a tiny white star on his chest and specks of white on the tips of both front paws, as if someone had just barely touched them with a small paintbrush. He was the largest black pup in the litter.

While the little one got to know his soon-to-be owner, Fred was busy checking the rest of the litter for another tailless wonder. "Well, the rest of them have tails, so that one was the only one shortchanged."

"Does Ms. Williams still have her Lab?" Tom asked, still holding the bobtailed baby.

"I guess, but I don't think he's the father; Ms. Williams lives over five miles from here."

"So that dog wouldn't be the first guy to go out of his way to see a girl, now would he?"

Both guys lost track of time as they enjoyed watching the puppies wrestle and play. Fred forgot about the hot meal he'd promised his wife. Even though he saw the puppies every day, this was his first time truly watching them.

"I think you made an impression," Fred said as he pointed at the little bobtailed pup sitting before them. The little guy never took his brown eyes off his human.

"I guess I did."

"So I think we have a winner; what are you going to name him?"

"Hold up. I haven't said which one I'm picking yet."

"Maybe you haven't decided yet, but that puppy has made up his mind. You could name him Nub." Fred laughed and approached the door of the pen.

Walking toward the pen's entrance, Tom stopped and returned the bobtailed pup to the ground, gently pushing him toward his brothers and sisters, but the puppy pushed back as if he knew they were about to leave without him.

"There you go, little man, go play," Tom said, trying to convince the little fellow.

"Come on, dude. If I hurry up, maybe I can at least get some meat on the grill before the wife gets home." After another minute or so, they finally made it through the pen door, leaving all the puppies on the other side.

Dodging chickens on their way back to Tom's truck, they discussed whether the puppies were old enough to be separated from their mother. Since the pups were still getting most of their food from nursing, both agreed it would be a good idea to wait another week before separating them.

"Okay, but you're missing your chance to get the pick of the litter," said Fred.

"I'll risk it," Tom replied.

Driving home, Tom still wasn't sure another dog would be a good idea. He didn't want to have Fred hold a puppy for him and then back out of the deal. At the same time, though, leaving that little bobtailed dog behind was hard for him.

"Oh well, I need to get home and feed the mutt I already have." He smiled as he thought about Lucky being mad because supper was late.

Lucky was a ten-year-old, twenty-pound spaniel mix that not only ruled the house but also believed he owned it. As Tom drove, he wondered how that old dog would feel about having a puppy in the house.

As demanding as Lucky could be at times, Tom cared for him as much as he had ever cared for a dog. His mom, Ms. Mary, had gotten Lucky from a family friend after his dad passed away. The little troublemaker was the only survivor out of a litter of six, hence the name "Lucky."

The word "spoiled" didn't entirely cover it. Nobody could get within three feet of Ms. Mary without Lucky's approval. The two were inseparable.

After about five years, Ms. Mary passed away, and Tom ended up with the little security guard. Lucky had meant so much to Tom's mom that taking him to a shelter or giving him to someone who didn't know him wasn't an option.

Tom lived in an old shotgun house that his grandmother had left him. Putting his key in the front door, he could hear his little roommate on the other side, barking as if he was telling him to hurry and get supper in his feed bowl. The old dog was fed almost every afternoon before five-thirty; if he wasn't, there was no peace to be had.

Walking through the front door without tripping over the little security alarm was a trick in itself. Lucky stood only about ten inches tall and, at best, sixteen inches long, but that didn't stop him from believing that he was ten-foot-tall and bulletproof. The little guy had no fear, and there was nothing he loved more than eating, and he knew that Tom walking through that front door meant it was supper time.

Nine Lives was on the menu. Yes, cat food, the small can was the perfect amount of food so there would be no leftovers but was enough to satisfy the hungry, little monster.

"Don't worry," Tom said with a smile as he set the bowl of food on the floor. "I'm not going to tell anyone that a vicious dog like you eats cat food every afternoon."

Lucky wasn't listening, too busy attacking his bowl like it had wronged him somehow.

Tom walked into the living room, still wrestling with the idea of getting another dog. It would be useful to have an outside dog, he thought. It could make someone think twice about stealing something from the yard or breaking into the house.

The noise of the feed bowl sliding around the kitchen floor as Lucky licked the bottom of it could be heard throughout the house. While he didn't care much for cats, the old dog felt very differently about cat food!

Leaning back in his recliner, Tom spent the next few minutes weighing the pros and cons of adding a dog to the yard.

"Lucky," he yelled. "How would you like a partner to help you protect the house when I'm not here?"

By then the old black spaniel had wandered into the living room without being noticed and crawled into his dog bed. Lying there full of cat food, Lucky was sound asleep, back feet twitching as if he was chasing something in his dream.

2

A HARD NIGHT

Two hours after they watched Tom's truck back out of the driveway, Marcy and Emma could still detect charcoal-flavored meat in the night air as they rested on Fred's back porch, expecting to sample what they were smelling. Having played this game before, they knew their patience would be rewarded at some point.

The sounds of plates and glasses clinking together in the kitchen sink kept the dogs at attention. Finally, the back door opened, and Fred walked out with two grilled hamburger patties in one hand and a hamburger bun in the other.

"Is this what you ladies have been waiting for?"

Both dogs pushed off with their front legs into a sitting position and wagged their tails with appreciation. Fred gave each dog a hamburger patty and split the bun between them.

"All right, girls, you may want to chew a little before you swallow," he said, but neither dog listened as they downed the meat and bun almost whole.

Fred decided to sit on the back porch while enjoying the peace and quiet of a country night. The only sounds in the air were the crickets in the distance and the occasional bray from Jack, a seven-year-old donkey standing in the pasture that consumed much of the backyard. Both of Fred's dogs were lying at the top of the porch steps, nodding off with full stomachs.

"Those two dogs," Fred thought. Even though there was a sizable age difference between them, Emma and Marcy had always been close. Fred had brought Marcy home when she was just a young puppy, and Emma treated her as her own.

Everywhere the big German shepherd went, the young Lab tagged along, ready to help. Marcy got to watch Emma fetch, swim and be a good watchdog, and it helped her learn the same duties.

After about an hour, Fred also started to nod off and decided it was time to call it a night. "Come on, girls." He stood from his rocking chair. "I bet we have some sleepy babies out there in that doghouse."

Every night before bed, Fred put Marcy in the dog pen with her puppies and let Emma decide whether she wanted to sleep in the enclosure with the Lab or out in the open. Some nights the shepherd followed Marcy right into the pen as if she couldn't wait to get in there, but tonight she kept her distance from the door.

"Suit yourself," Fred said.

Once the old dog saw her human disappear inside the main house, she turned and looked toward the pen as Marcy walked into the doghouse to bed down with her puppies.

About halfway between Fred's house and the pen on a thick patch of soft grass, the frail German shepherd decided she was in a comfortable spot to take her first nap of the night.

As she lay there with her eyes heavy, she could hear that she was surrounded by crickets chirping. There was also a night owl in the far distance asking a familiar question and a couple of bullfrogs in a neighboring pond trying to out-sing each other. Accustomed to these sounds from her many nights on the property, she followed them into a deep sleep.

As Marcy entered the doghouse, she stopped for a few seconds to give the inside a quick inspection, looking, listening and sniffing for anything different or out of place. This was a mother's instinct taking over, making sure that no unwanted visitors were near or inside the doghouse.

She turned her head toward the stack of puppies lying on top of the hay in one corner of the house, all fast asleep and peaceful. Suddenly she heard a whimper from the opposite corner; she quickly turned her head in that direction. It was the bobtailed pup standing on all fours by himself in the corner, waiting for his last meal of the day before going to bed. Unlike the other puppies in the litter, he made sure he wasn't going to miss it.

Marcy walked over to him and nudged him with her nose toward his brothers and sisters so each one would get an equal chance at some milk. After tripping over a few clumps of hay, he finally made it over to the other puppies. One by one the litter woke and realized that the dinner bell was ringing.

Marcy took her place beside the pups. As they fed, she bathed each one, licking it from head to toe and checking for strange smells or tastes.

As the Lab lay there watching over her litter, the pups stopped feeding one by one and fell asleep, exhausted from running and playing the day away inside the dog pen. The bobtailed pup was the last to give in to the Sandman, but when he fell asleep, an occasional puppy snore could be heard from his snout.

It was the perfect night for sleeping, cool but not cold, and the wind was so calm it was as if the woods surrounding Fred's house were asleep also. A few hours had passed; the two bullfrogs over at the neighbors' had called it a draw and stopped singing. The owl was nowhere to be heard, and even the crickets had toned down their noise.

Fred and his wife were dead to the world inside the house. Emma was also taking advantage of the conditions on the patch of grass she'd begun her night on, sound asleep and dreaming of days past when she was younger and more playful.

No sounds at all came from the dog pen. Marcy and the puppies were cuddled together in a wad, relaxed and unconscious.

Another hour passed before Emma woke from her deep sleep and raised her head, turning it from side to side as if she had forgotten where she was. After a few seconds, she was fully awake, but a very uneasy feeling came over her. The old German Shepherd felt that something had awakened her.

Not knowing what had disturbed her, she raised herself into a sitting position and listened. Ears up but hearing nothing out of the ordinary, Emma began to look around and survey the house, yard, and dog pen, watching for anything or any animal that didn't belong.

With nothing seeming out of place, she stood and began to walk toward the wood line.

Then it happened. It was a scent that Emma remembered smelling only a few times in her life but one that she could never forget. She did not know what it belonged to.

She stopped and sniffed the ground around her. There it was again: that smell that didn't belong in her yard. It was so different than the normal scents always around the farm. It wasn't human nor dog. No, this was something very different; this was a predator. This scent was from something dangerous, and she could tell it wasn't far away.

Emma let out three barks to warn whatever this creature was that she was aware of its presence and would not allow it. As she began jogging toward the dog pen, all her senses were on high alert.

She didn't know where this animal was, but the closer she got to Marcy and those puppies, the stronger its odor became.

Maybe it was the predator's odor or the adrenaline or a combination of the two, but in these moments, Emma's posture and movements changed. She forgot about her stiff joints and bad back; her senses were working overtime, and she had again become that young, powerful dog that once patrolled this property and controlled the animals allowed on it.

As the old shepherd reached the door of the pen, Marcy walked out of the doghouse with two of the puppies following behind her. Emma's barks had jarred Marcy from a sound sleep, and by now Marcy also had a snout full of the predator's smell.

Not recognizing the scent, the Lab let out three barks of her own to see if it would draw out a response from this unwanted visitor.

No answer came.

Both dogs stood in the silence and waited. Neither knew for sure what they were waiting for, but both had a very uneasy feeling about their immediate future.

After making sure that both pups that had followed her out of the doghouse were safely back inside, Marcy began to walk clockwise along the inside edge of the pen while Emma patrolled counterclockwise along the outside.

Suddenly, Marcy stopped and looked toward the wood line at the back of the property; she'd heard something. Not moving a muscle nor making a sound, she stared out across the backyard as if her whole body was frozen to the ground.

Not even taking a break to blink an eye, she stood like a statue, looking in the direction where the sound had originated. And then it happened; out of the wood line came the hungry predator, slowly but surely walking toward the pen with bad intentions hovering all around it.

It was bigger than a large dog, with yellowish eyes glowing in the dark and cat-like features. The opportunistic creature smelled something vulnerable. It had been lying and watching the property for some time, and it was tired of waiting for its meal.

Marcy started barking relentlessly at the animal while backing up toward the entrance of the doghouse. The cat-like creature was getting closer, ignoring the warning barks being sent its way.

As she backed up, the black Lab could feel the top of the doghouse entrance touching her back, and her hind feet were now inside the small structure. There was no more ground to give up as she stood there watching the predator get closer and closer to the pen.

By this time, her barks had become hoarse as she struggled to make them heard. She looked back over her shoulder at her puppies, then looked in the opposite direction toward the main house as if looking for guidance, but the help she hoped for from her humans was nowhere to be seen.

Fear, anger and the basic instinct to protect her puppies consumed Marcy's mind and body as she stood waiting for her opponent to reach her. She knew the fence wire separating her and her puppies from this monster would not be enough to stop it.

Still barking, she watched the calm and calculated hunter that was planning tonight's slaughter. She was now able to get a close view of the animal, and she hated what she saw.

Its yellow eyes, red tongue and large white teeth all seemed to glow in the dark as the monster moved closer and closer to the edge of the dog pen. This creature had been in similar situations like this countless times, and more times than not it got what it wanted.

Once at the edge of the pen, the big cat stood and fell forward, landing its two front paws on the fence and placing all the weight it could against the wire and the post it was nailed against. This method had worked for the big cat in the past, and he expected it to work again.

It only took a few blows for the wire and post to begin caving in toward the ground. One more time, the big monster lay into the fence with its front legs and paws, pushing it down to the ground while not taking its eyes off the doghouse.

Marcy stood her ground helplessly, watching the determined cat outsmart the dog pen. By now her warning barks had turned into something different. She was showing every tooth inside her head. Her fear had gone away; outrage and a mother's instinct had taken over. Instinct told her to protect those puppies, and anger gave her the courage to do so.

As the big cat cleared the post and wire and walked slowly toward the doghouse, Marcy noticed something in the darkness behind the cat. Suddenly, out of the blackness, the old German shepherd lunged forward with all the strength it could muster and landed on top of the cat, locking her jaws in the back of the hungry predator's neck.

The creature had been so focused on Marcy and the puppies that it had allowed Emma to do some stalking of her own and attack the monster from behind.

With Emma's teeth digging into the back of its neck, the cat stood up on its hind legs, supporting not only its weight but also the shepherd's. The cat let out a scream that echoed through the property as if it was rehearsed, but at this moment Emma neither saw nor heard anything.

With her eyes shut and her grip firmly planted in the big cat's hide, she believed she was fighting this monster to save not only her life but also the lives of every animal and human on the property. The old shepherd knew she had found a soft spot and had no plans of releasing it.

Violently, the cat slung Emma from side to side, trying to break her painful grip on the back of its neck, but not only was Emma not letting go, her teeth had also begun tearing through the cat's skin, and blood was trickling down its back.

Feeling the pain increase by the second, the cat landed its front paws back on the ground once more and, in desperation, used them to push off from the dirt and fall straight back, landing all its weight on top of Emma and crashing her into the ground.

The cat instantly felt relief. Eager to get a look at what it had been fighting, it quickly got back on all fours, anger filling its body and blood dripping down its neck. This was no longer just about food; now it was also about revenge.

Stunned, hurting and disoriented, Emma had lost the grip she had fought so hard to keep. Finding it hard to breathe and feeling the weight of her age in her muscles and joints, she slowly got to her feet. With blood from the intruder covering her mouth, she was now looking in the eyes of the most dangerous animal she had ever encountered.

There wasn't enough adrenaline left in the old German shepherd's body to make this a fair fight.

Marcy stood at the entrance of the dog pen and watched Emma do her best to stop the monster, but now she saw that same monster circling, almost taunting her, delaying what would be the second and final round of the fight that Emma was sure to lose.

Watching the angry cat size up the brave shepherd triggered something in Marcy. It was a panic, but a panic with intense rage. It wasn't just about protecting her puppies now. The more she watched the cat prepare to attack Emma, the angrier she became, and she began to bark again, loud and fast as if to tell the cat, "Hey, I'm over here, come get me," but the cat wasn't listening.

Marcy then heard a noise from the main house, followed by the sound of the front door shutting—a noise both Marcy and Emma had heard countless times. It was Fred, it had to be; finally, the help that Marcy had been waiting and watching for was on its way!

The big intruder also heard the noise and smelled a human getting closer. Willing to give up on its revenge but not so willing to give up on its food, the hungry cat turned and began to walk toward Marcy. Seeing this, Emma made one last attempt to stop the cat by grabbing one of its back legs, but at this point, she had neither the strength nor energy to pose a real threat to the big cat.

Pulling its leg free with a violent swing of its powerful body, the cat slapped Emma with one of its big front paws, lifting her off the ground and knocking her back several feet.

The back of Emma's neck hit the ground flush. She stayed on the ground, facing the cat, not knowing if her fight was over but realizing the fight in her was gone.

Understanding the inevitable, Marcy took her first step toward the monster. As the only obstacle between the cat and her puppies, she knew help was coming, but she also knew that Fred was too far away to stop the cat from reaching the doghouse.

Faster, stronger, and younger than Emma but lacking the element of surprise, Marcy could now smell the cat's breath as she took another step forward. She made firm eye contact just a split second before the cat lunged toward her, front claws first. The cat slapped Marcy across the side of her neck, cutting into her hide and knocking her back against the doghouse with such force that the house moved backward a couple of feet. Bleeding, Marcy quickly got back on her feet and stood before the doorway of the doghouse, ready for the next attack.

Sensing a kill, the cat regained its balance and lunged toward his prey once more. But Marcy was not as close to death as the cat had thought, quickly standing up on her back legs. The black Lab managed to catch the monster by the throat in midair and land on top of it, chewing into its already sore neck.

With her jaw locked in place, Marcy could feel the claws of the cat's hind feet digging into her stomach and sides. Using both hind legs, the cat made one big push, tossing Marcy up in the air and off to the side, causing her to lose the chokehold she had worked so hard for.

As the Lab landed back on the ground, she heard an explosion, then another and another.

It was Fred, running to the pen and firing his gun up in the air. He saw the big cat, and the big cat saw him. As the wounded hunter turned to run the other way, Fred aimed and fired, but the cat never stopped, disappearing quietly back into the woods from where it had come.

"Marcy!" Fred yelled as he stepped over the damaged fence. "You okay, girl?"

Marcy was lying there wagging her tail, happy to see Fred, but she was far from okay, bleeding from the scratches on her stomach and two deep cuts on her shoulder. She was a bloody mess.

With the help of his flashlight, Fred could see the damage. "Okay, girl, you are carved up pretty good, but the bleeding isn't as bad as it looks. Some of that blood must belong to that cat," Fred said. He took off his T-shirt and wrapped it around Marcy's back and stomach. "I'm going to get you to the vet."

"Emma?" Fred whispered to himself. He stood and looked around. "Emma!" he yelled into the darkness. After several seconds of silence, he heard a weak whimper off in the distance outside the dog pen perimeter. It was his old friend, lying on her side with all four legs stretched out in the same direction. He called out her name again, but the injured dog made no effort to move.

Fearing the worst, Fred ran to Emma's side. The closer he got to his dog, the more blood he could see and the more frightened he became. Emma had been part of the landscape around his home for a long time, not only protecting his property but also watching over his wife, kids, and other animals in her yard. She had become more than just a watchdog long before this night. She was part of the family.

As Fred reached the wounded German shepherd, he slowly kneeled and placed his hand on her side to see if she was breathing. She was almost unrecognizable because of the blood that covered her face and chest. Relief poured over him when he felt her heartbeat and realized that his hand was gently moving up and down as she breathed. Emma raised her head up, then slowly rested it back down on the ground. She was alive but exhausted.

Fred looked over Emma but surprisingly found only a few small cuts. The old German shepherd had given up her body to protect Marcy and those puppies.

"You did it, girl," Fred said, almost tearing up. "You protected us all tonight. I'm going to sit right here; you just lie there and rest."

The longer they sat there, the more unpredictable Emma's breathing became. Fred began to understand but hate what was happening. Gently rubbing the side of her face and neck, he thought back to the fat, clumsy puppy he had rescued from the pound eleven years earlier. "I almost decided not to bring you home that day," he said.

After another minute or so, the old shepherd's chest stopped moving. But even before that Fred could see the life escape from her face as she lay there looking at him. His tears soaked in the soil as he slowly pulled her collar from her neck.

Emma's last act had been her most selfless one. Without her, the death toll that night surely would have been higher. Because of her, those puppies would now have a chance to live a great life just as she had.

After Fred finished with Emma, he stood again and walked inside the dog pen to check on the puppies. Each puppy was sound asleep in a pile dead center of the doghouse.

3

A FORTUNATE PUP

On the way to Fred's, Tom stopped by the local feed and seed store and picked up everything he could think of to keep his new puppy happy for the weekend.

It had been a stressful Friday at the office, but he knew his friend was now desperate to find homes for those puppies.

As Tom eased up Fred's driveway, he realized how weird it was not to hear barking dogs escorting him up to the house.

Stepping out of his truck, Tom could see Fred repairing the dog pen that had been damaged the previous morning.

"So, that wire was no match for a big cat?" Tom asked as he got closer.

"I guess not," Fred answered. "But along with Emma, the fence slowed it down enough that I was able to get out here with my gun and chase it away. Without it, I think that cat would have killed both dogs and the puppies." Fred pulled a water-filled plastic bottle from his back pocket and drank half of it.

"When the morning began with me running across my yard with nothing on but a pair of work boots and a pair of boxers, I knew it would be an interesting day."

"Sorry about Emma. I know that's gotta hurt," Tom said.

Fred looked up and smiled. "Honestly, it hurts a lot, but whatcha gonna do? She died doing what she felt like she was meant to do. Judging from the amount of cat blood that was on her, she put up one hell of a fight."

Tom noticed a white wooden cross driven into the ground under a big pecan tree in the center of the backyard.

"So you've come to take three or four of those puppies off my hands, right?" Fred asked in a more cheerful tone.

Tom walked to the doghouse and looked inside; there was a pile of puppy cuteness lying in the middle of the house. The bobtailed pup was parked on the very top, fat, and content, almost snoring, the very front tip of its red tongue sticking out of its mouth.

On cue, the little pup's eyes began to open, and it saw Tom looking back. A big yawn happened just as the little guy managed to fully open both eyes.

"Where's Marcy?" Tom asked.

"To lessen the risk of infection, Doc Wright wanted to keep her until Monday. She's cut up pretty bad. The good news is her vaccination for rabies happened within the past year, so that shouldn't be a problem. Trying to decide which one to take?" Fred asked as he drove a new post into the ground.

"No, I know which one I want," Tom answered.

"Good. There is an empty box on the back porch that you can use to take him in. I don't mean to be a rude host, but I want to try to get this fence back up before dark. Then I need to decide what I'm going to do with the rest of those dogs. I can't let them stay out here by themselves with that cat still on the loose."

Tom, noticing how high the sun was, didn't think Fred would be able to finish before nightfall. "So you are redoing that corner section also?"

"Yep, that cat must have been strong. When it pushed this section down to make its way in, it also pulled the corner post down along with it."

Tom could tell it hadn't been an easy day for Fred. "Tell you what, if you promise me a cold glass of sweet tea and one of those hamburgers that you grilled last night, I'll stay and help you finish up."

"You sure?" Fred asked.

"Positive."

The guys spent the next hour or so making those fence posts and wire look like a dog pen again. Tom even managed to make Fred laugh out loud a few times.

"That should just about do it," Fred announced. He slammed the business end of the hole diggers into the dirt.

"Tom, I think I owe you a hamburger and a glass of sweet tea. Let's get these tools back in the shed and our hands washed."

By now all the puppies were awake and waiting along the fence.

"The dinner bell has rung inside those little heads," Fred said.

Arms loaded with tools, both men started walking toward the tool shed. Once inside, Fred led Tom to a corner and instructed him to prop up everything he had where he stood.

Also in the corner was a big, commercial-style sink they could use to wash their hands.

"Go ahead and wash up. I'm going to take a few cans of food back down to the puppies, and I'll meet you in the kitchen," Fred said.

Tom walked into the house and sat at the kitchen table; it had been a long day, he thought. Just a couple of minutes later, Fred walked in and headed straight for the refrigerator.

"I've been thinking about a grilled hamburger ever since I saw you lighting up the charcoal as I drove off last night," Tom admitted.

"Well, you are about to do more than just think about one," Fred joked. He laid a platter of meat on the kitchen counter before him.

"Where's the wife?" Tom asked.

"She's at her book club. They meet most Friday nights. So which puppy have you decided to take?"

"I think you already know which one—the bobtailed one," Tom answered.

"What are you going to name it?"

Tom hadn't even thought about a name yet. "Not sure. If those patties taste as good as they smell, I might name him Fred in your honor," he joked.

"You know, when I was a kid I had several dogs growing up, but the best dog I ever had was a beagle named Jasper. I loved that dog.

I had him about five years, I guess, and he just vanished one day. Never saw him again," Fred explained.

"Man, that's tough, losing a pet like that. Especially when you are a kid," Tom added.

"Yeah it was tough, I never found out what happened to him. For a while I didn't even want another dog, but our neighbor at the time felt so bad for me that he gave me a chocolate Lab puppy, and I named him Rex," Fred said.

"Hum, Rex, that sounds like a good name for a Lab. Rex the bob-tailed black Lab. I like it."

Tom had eaten two hamburgers and decided on a name for his new puppy before he finished his first glass of sweet tea. By the time both men finished eating, several stories about childhood pets had been told, and most of them were even true.

"Man, look at the time, I've got to go," Tom announced as he took one last swallow of tea before he stood from the kitchen table.

Both men walked out onto the back porch. After saying their goodbyes, Tom grabbed the cardboard box and started toward the pen to retrieve his new puppy. "That box has room enough for two or three," Fred yelled as Tom opened the gate to the pen.

Ignoring his host, Tom walked to the doghouse and looked in to find the little, fat, bobtailed pup back on top of the puppy pile. He laughed a little as he reached to grab the little guy and placed him inside the box.

"Don't worry, little fellow, this box is only temporary," Tom said. He closed the gate behind him and walked toward his truck.

When he reached the passenger-side door, he opened it and placed the box full of puppy on the seat. He then reached behind the seat and pulled out a yellow stuffed duck that had belonged to Lucky when he was a puppy. "Here you go, boy," he said, placing the toy beside him. The puppy was already asleep inside the cardboard box.

Tom had no way of realizing it, but this was the beginning of a long and lasting friendship.

4

HOMECOMING

Silence was interrupted by the bluebirds' occasional good morning and the mockingbirds living in the old oak tree outside Tom's bedroom window.

No traffic could be heard, no alarm clock screaming. Just pure and pleasant Saturday morning silence filled Tom's bedroom as he relaxed there, awake enough to see the sunlight starting to pour through the windows.

As Tom lay there getting his bearings, he could hear snoring from under the covers. "Some guard dog you are." Rubbing one eye, he noticed that there was still no movement underneath the blanket, but the snoring was getting louder. "My lord, that dog snores like a fifty-five-year-old man."

Finally, the lump in the covers started to move toward the head of the bed. Peeping through the edge, Lucky looked like a dog that had just woken up. He had always had a bedmate. This started with Ms. Mary. Now, Tom was reluctantly carrying on the tradition.

At first, he didn't have plans of ever letting Lucky sleep in his bed, but he quickly found out that it was hard to sleep inside a house with an unhappy dog that paced the floor all night.

Tom stayed in bed for what felt like ten minutes but was closer to thirty. A list of chores waited for him on the dining room table. He could only blame himself for the list, because he was the one who had written it.

The grass needed cutting, and the house needed a good cleaning. There was also a new member of the family inside the cab of his truck that needed some attention.

Driving home the evening before, he had decided to leave Rex inside the truck for the night. It was late, and the more he thought about it, the more he worried about Lucky not taking the news of a new puppy very well. He knew that an unhappy night for Lucky could mean a sleepless night for him.

He had lined the bottom of Rex's box with a couple of bath towels from inside the house and kept the windows cracked so the fresh, cool night air would fill the inside of the truck.

Just before he left the baby Lab, he saw one of his old shirts in the back seat.

"Here you go," he said. "You can get used to my scent while you sleep." He then used it to cover the little pup.

Tom wasn't sure how Rex felt about all this, but he could see the box held a tired little dog that could barely keep his eyes open.

After Tom lay in bed a few more minutes, he decided to stop delaying the inevitable. His feet hit the floor with purpose, then he headed to the kitchen to round up something for breakfast.

He found two pieces of cheese and part of a loaf of bread.

"Cheese toast it is," he said to himself. He put the two slices of bread covered with the two pieces of cheese into his toaster oven, set the timer, and decided to check on Rex while his breakfast heated up.

By the time Tom made it back to the bedroom, Lucky had climbed to the head of the bed and was sleeping with his head on one of the pillows.

"You sorry dog, I bet I've got something out in the truck that will make you get up," Tom bragged.

It was a chilly, crisp morning, but it was a good cool that made Tom want to be outside. Walking toward the truck, he looked for any signs of Rex through the truck windows.

Before he opened the truck door, Tom gazed inside to see what the little ball of fur was doing. He expected to find an unhappy puppy inside, waiting to be rescued, but what he saw happily surprised him.

It didn't appear that Rex had even moved during the night; he and the duck were still lying there just like the night before with Tom's shirt covering them.

Just as the truck door opened, the Lab puppy popped his little head above the side of the box and started wagging his nub.

"You are one brave, little dog," Tom said. He lifted Rex out of the box and placed him on the ground so the pup could take care of his business.

Once on the grass, the small Lab sat and looked all around as if he was soaking everything in.

"It's a different world, isn't it?" Tom asked.

After a minute or so of just sitting and looking, Rex finally stood and started to walk around and sniff everything in sight, but he was still careful not to get too far from his human.

"Go ahead, little man, get a good smell of the place."

After a few more minutes, Rex took care of his predictable business, then looked up at Tom as if asking what was next.

"That's it, boy, make yourself at home."

Eventually, Tom decided it was safe to take Rex inside the house. "Okay, let's go get Lucky out of bed," he said with a chuckle.

Holding Rex with one arm, Tom opened his front door and walked inside the house, swinging the door shut behind him. As he set the baby Lab down in the middle of the living room floor, Tom could hear Lucky's toenails hitting the kitchen linoleum as he played out his morning ritual of checking his food bowl first.

Tom sat on his knees beside Rex and called Lucky into the living room.

"Let's get this over with," he said to Rex and himself. Hearing Tom's call, the old black spaniel came running, expecting some breakfast to be waiting. Instead, he saw Rex staring back at him.

The closer Lucky got, the slower he ran until it became a careful walk, which then became what looked to be a protest sit-down about three feet from Rex and Tom.

After about ten seconds of silence, Tom said, "Come here, Lucky, and make friends with the little guy."

Lucky was motionless, ears straight up, staring a hole into the baby Lab. Then out of nowhere, Rex let out a little angry-sounding bark that startled both Tom and Lucky.

"Okay, kid, don't make this any harder than it has to be," Tom said.

After the warning bark from Rex, Lucky seemed to lose interest. He walked back into the kitchen to let out a bark of his own, reminding Tom that it was breakfast time and there was no food in his bowl.

Hearing Lucky bark made Tom remember that his breakfast was still in the toaster oven. "Well, at least he didn't try to bite you," he said.

After he and Lucky inhaled their breakfasts, Tom returned to the living room with a bowl and some cat food.

"I figured if it's good enough for the old man, it would be good enough for a little squirt," he said.

Rex had never eaten out of a bowl before but quickly got the hang of it.

The young Lab sat on the living room floor, watching his human get dressed while soaking up the inside of the house. As Rex sat there, Lucky walked in from the kitchen and carefully approached him as if not to spook the puppy or himself.

The small Lab didn't move a muscle as the old dog sniffed him from head to toe then began licking his face as if to give his approval. Rex returned the favor, and a friendship was born, although it would be a friendship with certain limitations, as the young Lab would learn as he got older.

"Glad to see you guys getting along," Tom said as he walked in from the bedroom and dropped his favorite pair of boots on the floor.

Rex's pallet sat on the living room floor along with a water bowl and an absorbent puppy pad. The plan was for the puppy to stay inside the house, and since Tom wasn't ready to trust Lucky to be alone with the baby just yet, the stubborn old dog would spend most of the day outside while Tom got his work done.

The puppy pad was hopeful thinking; there was no way of knowing whether Rex would use it, so Tom stopped what he was doing every so often to take the baby Lab outside for a bathroom break.

The young Lab seemed more satisfied outdoors. There were more sights to see, more smells to smell, and more noises to hear, and he was curious about all of it, bouncing around from one attention-getter to another.

While the day passed, Tom's to-do list became smaller and smaller. The grass was cut, the truck washed, and both porches hosed down. As each job was checked off the list, Lucky supervised from under one of the big oaks, watching his partner's every move and making sure nothing and no one set foot on the property without being announced.

A wet T-shirt was proof that the chilly morning had given way to a warm afternoon. As Tom drove the lawn mower back into the old shed in the backyard, he looked down at his watch to check the time. He had spoken earlier that day to Hope, who was supposed to show up around five o'clock to grill out.

Hope and Tom were an on-again, off-again couple. Tom wasn't sure if they were on or off right now because at times, the two situations seemed to overlap. It was complicated, but more so for him than Hope. See, Tom had always veered away from hard commitments. He didn't like the term "girlfriend," but she was a good friend, and she was a girl—an attractive, sweet and caring woman who scared him to death at times.

While Tom walked back toward the house, Lucky met him halfway and started walking back with him as if to hurry him up.

"Now what do you have on your mind?" Tom asked. "I bet you're wondering what that little dog is up to; let's go check on him."

Tom trotted up the front porch steps with Lucky in tow, opened the front door and found Rex dead to the world, fast asleep on his pallet.

"Man, that baby is a heavy sleeper. You know, Lucky, I remember you were a whiny little mess at that age," Tom said.

Lucky, paying no attention to Tom nor the puppy as usual, headed straight for the kitchen to check his feed bowl and get a drink of fresh water.

The warm day gave way to a gorgeous afternoon in Tom's front yard. The tall oaks were providing plenty of shade, the grill was getting hot, and the pork chops and hamburger patties were seasoned, ready to cook.

The two dogs sat on the front porch, enjoying the smells from the grill. Lucky knew what was about to happen; the young Lab wasn't so sure, but he knew he liked what he smelled so far.

Tom went inside the house and came back with a pack of hot dogs. "Who wants a grilled hot dog?"

The words "hot dog" automatically made Lucky's tail wag.

Tom looked down at his watch and wondered what was keeping Hope. He reached for his cell phone, but just as he was about to dial her number, a car could be heard getting closer and closer.

"How's that for timing," he said to himself as he watched Hope pull into his driveway. Finally, what he had been waiting for and working toward all day was about to happen: some alone time with his girl.

Tom yelled out to Hope to see if she needed help carrying the food she'd brought for the cookout.

"No, I think I got it," she answered. "You just keep watching that grill. I didn't come over here to eat burnt pork chops tonight."

Once Lucky realized it was Hope in the yard, he ran to the gate to meet her. Tom had always joked that Lucky would fight two pit bulls to get into Hope's lap, and while that may have been an exaggeration, there was no doubt that Lucky had made a connection with her.

Hope managed to open the gate door and step around Lucky without dropping the green salad and dessert she had prepared. She set the food on a small patio table that Tom had set up on the porch.

"I've got to go back to the car and get Vito," she said.

"You brought the cat?" Tom asked.

Vito was a ten-pound, half-Persian, half-nobody-could-be-sure cat that Hope had saved from the shelter a couple of months earlier. The cat may have been fifty percent Persian, but it was one hundred percent attitude and always acted like it was in a bad mood.

Tom named it Vito due to its bad attitude and black coat with white markings that made it appear to be wearing a tuxedo.

"Yep, I brought the cat. I don't think he feels good," Hope replied.

"Really, how could you tell?" Tom asked, half-joking.

"Well, he didn't eat this morning, and right before we left home he coughed up a furball. He's been stuck inside the house all week, so I thought being outside with some fresh air might do him some good."

Hope turned around and headed back toward the car to get the grumpy cat.

"Lucky, this might not be a relaxing afternoon for you after all," Tom said as he kneeled to scratch Lucky's back.

Lucky and Vito had never really seen eye to eye on things. Lucky enjoyed being the boss while Vito enjoyed not having a boss, so the two never really became friends.

Once, the old dog tried to force the issue at Hope's house and received a claw mark on his nose for his trouble. Vito was the only animal Lucky had ever been around that was more stubborn than he was. To say that Vito didn't care for dogs that much would be an understatement. It didn't help that both animals wanted and loved attention from Hope.

Hope walked up the steps and set Vito down in one of the rocking chairs on the porch. Now, if you set most cats down in a strange place where there was a dog, you might have to worry about them being nervous or running up the nearest tree, but not with Vito. That cat lacked neither self-confidence nor courage and had no problem showing it.

Tom and Hope walked into the house to get the pork chops and something to drink. Lucky, realizing that Vito was on the porch and knowing the cat was sensitive about his personal space, stood at attention but never made a move toward the cat. Rex, on the other hand, didn't know any better and was about to learn his lesson the hard way.

Vito was the first cat the curious pup had ever seen, and curiosity was getting the better of him. Rex aimed a bark in the cat's direction, but Vito ignored the little guy. Rex barked a second time but still saw no movement from the cat.

Vito's unresponsiveness made the little puppy even more curious. Finally, unable to take it any longer, Rex walked up to the bottom of the chair Vito was in, sat down and barked a third time, demanding to be noticed, but the cat still wouldn't look his way.

Meanwhile Lucky had eased into a lying position to enjoy his front-row seat to this show. By this time, the small Lab had become aggravated apart from being curious, so he stood on his little hind legs and placed his front paws on the chair's bottom leg to let out a fourth bark. The fourth time got the cat's attention.

Before Rex could even recover from the bark, Vito with lighting speed slapped the little pup across the face with his right front paw, knocking him back onto the floor of the porch. It was almost as if Vito had lured Rex into striking distance before firing the shot.

Rex, having no idea that anything could move that fast, did the only thing he could do: he got up and ran as fast as possible away from the crazy cat, crying and yelping as he stumbled down the front porch steps.

Tom, hearing the commotion, swung the front door open just in time to see the pup running underneath the front porch for protection. He looked over at Vito, who sat in the rocking chair licking his right front paw as if nothing had occurred.

Hope, hearing Rex's cry for help, followed Tom out of the house. "What happened?"

"I think Rex got too close for Vito's comfort," Tom answered.

"Vito, you bad cat!" Hope scolded.

Vito, having no reaction to Hope's words, continued sitting in the rocking chair and licking his front paw, seemingly unaware of what just took place.

Tom laid his drink down on the table, "I hope he stopped running before he got too far underneath the house," he said as he walked down the steps to fetch his puppy. Reaching the edge of the front porch, he bent to one knee and began looking for Rex. By now the little pup had stopped crying and was quiet as a church mouse beside the farthest corner pillar under the porch.

"Hey, little guy, I guess you found out the hard way that Vito isn't very friendly."

There was no way Tom could reach the pup with his arm, so he started calling out, hoping to get the little guy to come closer, but that plan didn't work either.

Hope stood behind Tom, enjoying every minute of his failure. "Well, looks like you are going to be crawling under there to get him," she said.

"You sound pretty sure of yourself, lady," Tom said as he stood back up.

"Well, you can't leave him under there. He's scared to death," Hope replied.

"You are extremely cute when you get serious. Hold that thought."

Tom then turned and walked back up onto the front porch, grabbed a pork chop and hurried back down with a big smile.

"So, this is your plan?" Hope asked.

"Have you noticed how chubby that little pup is? He loves to eat, so I'm guessing it's going to be hard for him to turn down this treat once he gets its scent up his nose."

The plan worked. Lying on his back, Tom threw a piece of the meat in Rex's direction. It landed about six inches from the little pup's feet. Slowly Rex began to move forward, and once he was close enough, he gobbled up the piece of meat.

Tom repeated this two more times. He then quickly grabbed the Lab puppy and pulled him to daylight.

"That cat must be going soft. He didn't even leave a mark. You got off easier than Lucky did when he first met that crazy cat," Tom joked.

The rest of the afternoon went according to plan. Hope and Tom spent some much-needed and deserved time together; Rex spent the afternoon being passed back and forth between Tom's and Hope's laps and loving every minute of the attention.

Lucky spent the afternoon eating wieners and chewing on pork chop bones, while Vito spent most of the afternoon in the rocking chair where Hope first laid him, acting neither interested nor amused by anything going on around him.

Although it was exactly what Hope and Tom had wished for, the afternoon passed quickly. Before they knew it, they were sitting in the old front porch swing with the only light being from the moon and the only sounds from the coyotes in the distance.

"You know, it's a little odd when you think about it," Hope said, looking into Rex's shiny, brown eyes.

"What's that?" Tom asked.

"Everything about this little guy is perfect. His ears, legs, feet, coat—everything is exactly how and where it is supposed to be, minus one tail. Does that not strike you as odd?"

"I think 'interesting' is a better word for it. We did find out a few things about the little guy today. Because of Vito, he's most likely not going to like cats."

"The second thing we figured out is he loves sweet potatoes," Hope added.

"Sweet potatoes?"

"Yep, you haven't noticed me feeding him sweet potatoes all

afternoon. I found them in your refrigerator, brought them out here thinking Lucky would eat them, but Rex wolfed them down."

A few more minutes passed, and Hope announced that it was time for her and Vito to head home. Although Tom hated to see her leave, he was exhausted. It had been a long day.

Lucky and Rex watched Tom and Hope say their goodbyes from the front porch, lying side by side and waiting to see what would happen next.

Going to bed was Tom's plan as he walked up the porch steps. He reached down and picked up Rex. "Come on, guys, let's call it a night. My bed is calling my name."

5

YARD DOGS

Monday morning came fast.

Rex and Lucky sat on the front porch as they watched Tom back down the driveway for work. Today would be a first for both of them. It would be their first time home alone together—no Tom or Hope, just the two pups in a big, fenced-in yard.

Lucky had tolerated Rex all weekend. He allowed the curious Lab to tag along to a certain degree, but when Lucky grew tired of a side-kick, he would pick up his pace and leave the little guy behind. After a while, he would let Rex catch back up. For now, Lucky controlled the amount of contact he had to endure with Rex, but that control would not last forever.

Not much could happen in or around Tom's yard to surprise the little black spaniel. He had scratched or sniffed on every inch of the yard surrounded by the chain link fence. Rex, on the other hand, was full of wonder, new smells and new sounds, and he wanted to explore but also felt the need to stay close to Lucky, who had never been around a younger dog and had lost the last bit of puppy in him years ago.

Now the fence and everything inside the yard belonged to Lucky, or at least that's what the old spaniel believed. He also took it as a personal insult if another dog got near his fence; this happened oc-casionally when customers from the gas station next door walked their dogs close to the property line. As fate would have it, about ten minutes into Rex's first day alone with Lucky, a full-grown Doberman stepped up to the fence and started sniffing and scratching the ground around it.

Lucky saw this from his perch on the front porch and immediately sounded the alarm, letting four or five barks out as a warning to the visitor. When the signal went unnoticed, Lucky quickly ran down the steps and toward where the intruder stood.

The Doberman, to his credit, didn't flinch or bark back as he calmly stood there and watched Lucky pitch a good fit from the other side of the property line. Once the old dog decided that he had made his point, he hiked up one of his hind legs and gave the bottom of the fence a good spraying. He then turned and walked back to the porch and up the steps to claim his spot beside Rex.

This scenario happened two or three times a day, sometimes with dogs, sometimes with people. Each time, Rex sat back and watched as Lucky defended his ground. For Lucky, it was all about letting any dog or human know they were now on his territory.

After a few days of soaking all this in, Rex became brave enough to follow his mentor to the property line and get a ringside seat to the show Lucky put on for visitors. The Lab puppy sat as the old dog scratched, barked and strutted. This was his way of claiming ownership of the grounds.

After a couple of months or so passed, Tom decided one Saturday morning that it was past time to take Rex to the veterinarian for his first checkup.

"Time to go meet Dr. Wright," he mumbled, picking Rex up off the front porch. It was also time for Lucky's yearly checkup, so the old spaniel reluctantly joined the trip.

Dr. Wright was a colorful veterinarian who had practiced in Oakville for years. Originally from Oakville, he had run away from home at fifteen to work on shrimp boats in Bayou La Batre. At sixteen, he lied about his age and joined the army. After basic, the young soldier trained to be a medic and received an all-expenses-paid trip to Korea.

During the war, he treated countless men on the battlefield and earned a Purple Heart. "I've heard it called a conflict, but it looked, felt and smelled like war to me," he would say.

When his time in the army ended, he wanted to continue working in the medical field but had gotten his fill of seeing people suffer, so with help from the GI Bill, he attended Auburn University and later attended the Auburn University School of Veterinary Medicine, where he earned his degree.

Dr. Wright always said that animals were smarter than humans and better patients.

Tom walked into the office with Rex hooked to a leash in one hand and the end of Lucky's chain in the other. It was a rule that any animal inside that office, no matter how big or small, had to be secured so they couldn't run away or hurt another animal. The red collar that Rex wore was too big for his neck, but it served the purpose for that day.

"Be careful. That collar is trying to swallow that puppy," a deep voice said from the corner of the waiting room. It was the old doctor, sitting in one of the neglected office chairs and holding a newspaper with an unlit cigar in his mouth.

"There's my little buddy named Lucky," Dr. Wright added.

"How are ya, Doc?"

"I'm hanging in here like a hair in a biscuit."

"Well, you don't look too busy. What's with the unlit cigar?" Tom asked as he stuck out his hand for a shake.

"This is me saying enough is enough. I've decided that if Korea couldn't kill me, and my first wife's cooking didn't kill me, I won't let these cancer sticks do it," the old doctor explained.

Ordinarily, Dr. Wright's office stayed full because he saw more than just animals. Unofficially, a third of his patients were people. He had been in Oakville so long that everybody knew his history, and some people trusted him with their medical problems as much as they did the family doctor in town.

Broken bones, gout, rashes, common colds, sprain ankles, infections, and snake bites were all things he had treated as an army medic, so if someone came to him and needed help but didn't have the money to see the family doctor, then the old army medic did what he could. Payment might be just a "thank you," or it could be a jar of homemade jelly or a freshly baked cake.

Now 'doctor' would not be the first word that came to mind upon meeting Dr. Wright for the first time. 'Unkempt' would be a polite way to put it. Long gray beard, messy hair, faded blue jeans and a faded T-shirt. He didn't look the part of a doctor, but there wasn't a better veterinarian in the state.

"This is a fine Lab puppy you have here, Tom," Dr. Wright said as he took the pup and walked into the exam room. "Okay, I'll take some blood and run some quick tests, then give him his vaccinations."

He left the room and came back a few minutes later with good news. "All is good with his blood work," he announced.

"Would you say he is a full-blooded Lab?" asked Tom.

Dr. Wright grabbed his stethoscope off the hook on the wall and listened to Rex's heart and stomach. He then looked inside each ear and checked his teeth and gums. "I can't say for certain, but I wouldn't care if he is full-blooded or not. From the looks of it, he's a beautiful, healthy puppy that will grow up to be an exceptional dog. However, I am curious about one thing. How many puppies were in his litter?"

"There were eight," Tom answered.

"How many were bobtailed?" the old doctor asked.

"He was the only winner in that category."

"Okay, Mr. Rex, let's get your weight, and you will be all done here," Dr. Wright said as he gently placed Rex on the scale. The Lab puppy never fussed nor cried during the poking, the feeling, or even the shots, acting very brave throughout the visit.

"Tell me something, Tom. How does Rex feel about water?" Dr. Wright asked.

"Water?" Tom answered, sounding confused.

"Yeah, have you seen if he likes to swim yet?" Dr. Wright replied.

"Oh yes, that dog loves the fishpond."

If someone mentioned the word 'pond,' the black Lab gave his full attention. Tom joked that Rex should have been born with gills and fins.

The thirty-foot pier that extended into the water was Rex's launching pad. His favorite thing to do in the whole world was getting a running start at the end of that pier, scampering the full length of it, and leaping off the edge into the water. Most dogs at that age might have been timid about making those jumps, but not Rex.

Tom enjoyed watching the excited Lab run that pier almost as much as the dog enjoyed doing it. The black Lab acted as if he could fly. With each week that went by, Rex's jumps covered more and more distance.

"Sounds to me like we have a prime candidate for this year's Jumpathon," Dr. Wright added.

The Jumpathon was a charity event that raised money for the Oakville animal shelter. Dogs that were trained jumpers from all over the southeast would come to compete. To make it more interesting for the Oakville residents, there was also an amateur class that included mainly local dogs. The winner of the amateur competition automatically qualified for the finals, earning a chance to compete against the trained jumpers on the last day of the competition.

"I haven't thought about entering him, but it sounds like a good idea," Tom said.

"Well, the next Jumpathon is only five months away so he's not going to be old enough to compete in that one but keep putting him on that pier so he can train," Dr. Wright said as he handed Rex back to Tom.

"I owe that boy a treat for being so brave today," Dr. Wright announced. He reached under the exam table and pulled out a box of treats. "Here are four, so he and Lucky can each have another one later."

Tom picked Lucky up and placed him on the exam table. The old spaniel wasn't as friendly about the exam as Rex. Dr. Wright knew from past experience that a muzzle would be needed for this patient to prevent any bloodshed.

"Okay, Mr. Lucky, I won't bite you, so I'm not gonna let you bite me," Dr. Wright explained as he placed the muzzle around his mouth. He started his routine of listening, sticking, and feeling.

"Any concerns with Lucky? Is he eating and drinking water as he should?" Dr. Wright asked as he walked back into the room.

"He might be a little slower than he used to be, but he seems to be doing fine."

"Lucky, us old folks have to stick together," Dr. Wright said as he lifted him on the scale.

"Well, everything looks and sounds good, and his blood work looks normal. It wouldn't hurt him to lose a couple of pounds, but a lot of us fall into that category," Dr. Wright explained.

"Okay, we have got to get out of here. I've got things to do today. How much do we owe you?" Tom asked.

"I'll mail a bill to you," Dr. Wright replied.

Tom's schedule didn't allow him a lot of time with Rex other than on weekends, so Lucky became a vital source of information for the pup. Over the next few months, the performances at the fence weren't the only lessons Lucky would give Rex.

Whether he meant to or not, Lucky became a teacher of all things dog, and Rex was a good student. When to expect to be fed, when and how to patrol the yard, where to go during a thunderstorm. He showed him the coolest places on the property during the summer and the warmest places during the winter.

Rex watched everything Lucky did, and even though he tried to emulate most of it, his personality was different. Both had a confidence about them, but Rex was a gentler, more loving dog.

The young Lab wasn't as quick to warn visitors to stay off his territory, although he would if he felt the need. Because of this, he would become an exceptional watchdog. When Tom heard Rex bark, he knew the barking wasn't just for show, so he paid more attention to it.

Rex and Lucky's relationship didn't consist only of Rex trying to pattern his behavior after Lucky's. Rex learned some hard lessons as a puppy that he would carry with him for a long time. One was that Lucky's feed bowls were off-limits, which he learned the hard way, resulting in him running underneath the front porch to take cover several times.

Another lesson was about horseplay. Rex loved to pick at the old dog. It was one of his favorite forms of entertainment, but he learned to do it from a safe distance. Again, this was taught the hard way.

Through lessons taught and lessons learned, Rex grew to rely on Lucky and look at him for guidance. Even after Rex outgrew him in size, Lucky was still the boss.

6

PATCH

Pine trees and more pine trees. That's what Tom saw as he and Rex walked over his property, heading toward what sounded like a large piece of equipment moving around behind his house.

It was just after daylight on a Sunday morning, and he wasn't expecting these types of noises. However, Tom had contacted a local logger a few days earlier about thinning some pine trees, so he assumed the sound came from a piece of the logging equipment.

If the noises from the machinery bothered Rex, he was doing a great job of hiding it. The black Lab loved to walk amidst the tall, green pines and discover fresh scents to smell and new sounds to hear. He also made it a point to mark his territory as much as he could to let other dogs in the area know those pines trees belonged to him.

As Tom and Rex got closer to the sounds, they could see a glimpse of what was causing them; it was the logging crew foreman driving a large skidder, clearing out a spot to park the tree loader.

Tom wasn't expecting the logging crew to start so fast. He planned to walk over the whole property to get an idea of how many loads of trees to expect from the cutting before the crew started.

He decided that morning to go ahead and walk around the property and count trees. When Tom was younger, he had done some timber cruising on the side to make extra money, so it wouldn't take him long to get an idea of how many loads of wood to expect.

It seemed Rex was stopping at every third tree, sniffing, looking and scratching. Lucky had taught him well. Rex was now around six months old and growing like a healthy weed, no longer needing Lucky's help to find his way around. Week by week, he was transforming from a cute puppy into a beautiful, young Lab.

Rex had no idea why their walk was lasting longer than usual, but he was taking advantage of the opportunity. Making the adventure even better was the fact that every so often Rex spooked a rabbit or squirrel that jumped out of the weeds covering the ground under the pines.

The energetic dog ran back and forth between Tom and the area that the skidder was working, almost inviting the foreman to follow him. Along the way, he stopped to investigate anything that looked or smelled interesting.

Rex was very curious about everything, and he used his nose to touch, sniff and move around objects that he wanted to learn more about. Hope would tell him that his nose was going to get him in trouble one day.

Tom wasn't paying much attention to the young Lab; he was busy looking at trees. Rex, however, made sure to keep his master within seeing distance, never letting him get too far.

Having about as much fun as a young dog could without getting into trouble, Rex was happy being out of that yard for a change. Being able to run full speed without a fence in the way felt great. He was full of energy, and he enjoyed being able to get rid of some of it.

After roaming around for over an hour, the young Lab started looking for a place to sit and rest. Knowing the general direction Tom was heading, he ran up ahead and lay down in a clearing to wait for him. He could still hear the skidder working off in the distance.

After lying there a few minutes, Rex noticed an unrecognizable scent. He heard the rustling of pine straw under one of the trees about fifteen feet away. The black Lab turned his nose up in the air to see if he could catch the scent again.

Full of curiosity, the young dog got up and approached the sound. Noticing that the noise from the skidder was getting easier to hear, he could see the pine straw move at the base of the tree; this made him stop and stare at the ground directly beneath the tall pine. The intrigued Lab then sat and let out a playful bark.

After waiting several seconds for a response that never came, he decided to walk closer. As he closed in on the tree, a tiny paw could be seen digging out from under the straw.

It was a newborn of some sort. Rex immediately began to bark and run circles around the tree. The Lab still had a lot of puppy in him, so it didn't take much to excite him.

The more the little paw worked in the straw, the more amazed Rex became. A leg became visible in the straw, then a shoulder, then the head. By this time, Rex had sat down in front of the movement in the straw, wagging his nub and watching to see what would happen next.

In the meantime, the skidder was getting closer; using its front blade to push down anything in its path, the foreman was now making a road on the property for the other equipment to use once it arrived.

Tom was about eighty yards away in a steep gulley and could see Rex sitting there, looking at the tree, but he couldn't see what was holding his attention.

He noticed Rex was in the skidder's path, but it was clear the Lab was paying attention to nothing but the bottom of that pine tree.

Tom yelled at the young pup to get his attention.

Rex looked up from his trance and saw the skidder heading toward him. He turned back to Tom and started barking.

Tom yelled at him again to get out of the way, but Rex wouldn't move.

The Lab turned his attention to the skidder and started running toward it. By this time Tom knew something wasn't right, so he started climbing the steep hill toward the skidder also.

The foreman was paying attention only to the brush and small trees he was plowing through. He did not see the dog running at him.

Once Rex was about twenty feet away from the blade plowing toward him, he stopped, kneeled with his front legs and started barking and growling with everything he had at the skidder. As the big piece of machinery moved forward, Rex backed up at a slower pace.

Before Tom knew it, his dog was about a car's length away from the front blade. The young dog was now standing on all fours, and his two front feet jumped off the ground with each bark. Tom was working hard, pulling himself out of the deep gulley, trying to reach the foreman.

Between the noise coming from the engine and the debris stuck and hanging from the front skidder blade, the foreman still couldn't see or hear Rex, but the half-grown dog was doing all he could to get his attention.

Tom yelled again, begging Rex to get out of the skidder's way, but it did no good; the Lab was determined to somehow stop the giant monster from getting to that newborn. Tom yelled again, this time at the foreman, but his words went unheard.

Finally, he remembered that the foreman's cell number was programmed in his phone. Completely out of breath, he stopped, grabbed the phone from his pocket, found the number and dialed it.

"I hope he has it with him," he said to himself.

The foreman answered on the third ring.

"Hello."

"Stop the skidder!" Tom yelled.

"What?" asked the foreman.

"Stop the skidder!"

"Who is this?"

"It's Tom, and you are about to run over my dog!"

The foreman immediately shut down the piece of equipment.

Tom hung up and took a deep breath. The danger of the blade reaching Rex was over, but now he wanted to kill the young Lab for putting him through the last three minutes.

"What was that crazy dog thinking?" Tom asked himself.

Once the skidder stopped moving, Rex ran back to the pine tree that the baby animal was beneath. By this time, the painfully weak animal had moved away from the tree and was sitting up, yelping. Rex stopped and sat facing the small creature as if he was pointing at it.

Tom finally made it up the hill as the foreman climbed off the skidder.

"Sorry, I didn't see the dog until I killed the engine; what was he doing?"

"I don't know, but it looks like he's found something at the bottom of that pine," Tom explained.

"Reckon it's a snake?"

"Maybe. Let's go check it out."

As they walked closer, Rex began to bark and walk circles around the pup.

"I bet it's a rattlesnake," the foreman said.

"I kinda wish you would stop saying that, since neither of us has a gun," Tom said.

"Sorry."

The closer they got to Rex, the more excited the young Lab became.

"What is that?" the foreman asked.

"Well, it's not a snake. I believe it's a puppy," Tom said, sounding relieved.

Tom lowered himself to one knee and looked the tiny pup over. Then, using only one hand, he picked it up and stood. "I wonder what kind of dog it is?"

The foreman stepped toward Tom. "Not sure, but it's a boy. Its eyes are not even open yet; it could be a coyote, or it could be part-dog, part-coyote. That would explain it being out here in the woods."

"If we move him, he will need to be bottle-fed for a while. Do you have a dog?" Tom asked.

"No," the foreman answered quickly. "And there is a good reason why. You know how some ladies would love to take a puppy and feed it and love it and take care of it? Well, my wife is not one of those ladies. Half the time, she doesn't even want me in the house. Besides, what makes you so sure that its mom isn't coming back for him?"

Tom looked around and stepped closer to the tree. He bent and started raking at the pine straw. "This is how I know," he answered.

The foreman watched as Tom gently pushed straw off three dead puppies.

"It's common for one or two puppies in a litter to end up bigger than the rest because they fight harder for the milk. He's poor now, but I bet this little guy was the fattest one in this litter," Tom explained.

"So you think the other three starved to death?" asked the foreman.

"I think so. There are no marks on them, and they are nothing but skin and bones. My guess is they went to sleep and never woke up."

While Tom and the foreman stood there solving the mystery of the dead puppies, Rex sat under the two men and quietly scratched at the pine straw that surrounded the little animals as if he was trying to wake them up. The dog was seeing death for the first time in his young life, but it wouldn't be the last.

"So do you have any ideas for the little guy you are holding?" the foreman asked.

Tom thought for a few seconds. "Well, we can't leave it out here. I know a guy that owes me. I took this Lab off his hands, and he's about to return the favor. He just doesn't know it yet."

"Well, good luck. I've got to get back to work," the foreman said as he walked back to the skidder.

Still holding the hungry puppy, Tom leaned down and scratched Rex's neck with his free hand.

"You found me something to do today, didn't you, boy?" Tom asked as Rex reached up and tried to lick his face.

Tom stood again and started walking home but stopped when he realized he was walking alone. He called out to Rex, who was still sitting with the three dead puppies. Seeing this, Tom walked back to the pine tree, pulled his hunting knife from its holster, and began to dig.

Once he was satisfied with the size of the hole, he placed the three little ones inside and covered them with dirt and straw. After he finished, he took his finger and tugged on Rex's collar.

"Come on, boy, we need to see if this little guy will eat. I'd rather not have to dig another grave today."

Tom drove up Fred's driveway with Rex on the back of his truck and the newborn puppy covered with a bath towel inside the cab.

Fred was sitting on his front porch with a syringe waiting for them.

"So Rex found a coyote?" he yelled, stepping off the front porch.

"Honestly, it's going to have to grow some before we can tell what it is. Right now, I'm worried we may not get the chance to find out if we don't get some milk in its stomach."

Tom handed the puppy to Fred, who immediately put the business end of the syringe inside its mouth. The tiny pup was so weak that Fred had to pry its little mouth open with his fingers. He slowly pushed three or four drops of milk through the syringe, hoping the puppy would taste it and want more.

Unable to see, the newborn started grabbing for the syringe with its legs and paws as it tasted the milk.

"We have a winner! We are going to need a bottle," Fred said.

He told Tom where to find the baby bottles inside his garage. "Hurry up, he's trying to eat the syringe," Fred yelled as he stood there, happy that the puppy was taking the milk.

"What kind of milk are you feeding it?" Tom asked.

"Well, after you called, I realized I didn't have anything that would work. You can't just pull the gallon of sweet milk out of the refrigerator and give it to a newborn puppy. So I jumped in the truck and drove down to a neighbor's house and borrowed some fresh goat milk. I figured if it was good enough for a baby goat, it should work for this little guy."

Fred filled the bottle with the goat milk and secured the cap. He dropped a couple of drops on his wrist.

"That's still warm enough," he said, pointing the nipple in the direction of the pup's little mouth.

Fred didn't have to coax the little guy to try the bottle's nipple. The newborn latched on to it like it had been sucking from that bottle all of its short life.

"How about that," Tom said.

Tom walked around to the tailgate of his truck to let Rex to the ground. He immediately jumped down once the tailgate was open. The playful Lab ran around the property, expecting to be greeted by Marcy.

Once he realized he was the only dog on the property, he went to where Tom was standing and sat beside him.

"Look at that; Rex knows who his master is," Fred said. "The wife took Marcy to Dr. Wright this morning. How have you liked having a Lab around?"

"I'm fine with it. I don't think Lucky liked the idea at first, but he eventually came around."

The newborn puppy's belly had begun to swell with the milk it was taking in.

"Okay, I think that's enough. So Tom, what are you going to name it?" Fred asked.

"I'm going to let you decide that," he answered.

"Me? Oh no, I'm happy to help you this morning, but I don't need another animal right now," Fred said with a stern voice.

"Look, you have raised puppies from a bottle before, it's second nature for you. You already have a doghouse inside a pen, so you have a safe place for it to stay," Tom argued.

Fred stood there, holding the puppy in one hand and the milk bottle in the other. He thought for a few seconds, then looked at Tom. "Okay, I'll make a deal with you. I'll keep the little guy until I know he can eat solid food, then he belongs to you."

Tom smiled and agreed. He knew that if Fred kept the puppy long enough, he would fall in love with it and be unable to complete the deal.

"Did you notice that one of his eyes looks like it may be damaged?" Fred asked as he gave the puppy an inspection.

Tom walked back toward Fred and eyeballed the puppy also.

"I didn't notice, but I see it now. Looks like he may have a black spot of hair over that eye. It's going to look like a patch over it. Maybe you should name him Patch," Tom suggested.

"Patch. I like it," Fred agreed.

Tom backed out of Fred's driveway that morning knowing he had left that little animal in good hands. He also knew there was very little chance that he would ever have to live up to the deal he and Fred just made.

7

CHURCH

Just like every other Sunday morning, Ms. Faye Logan walked through the two massive doors of the First Baptist Church of Oakville two hours before the morning service started. She was always the first person there, beating the pastor by an hour and everyone else by at least an hour and a half.

She had become a member of the church as a little girl. She could remember running around and playing in the churchyard as a child.

Even though her parents didn't attend many Sundays, they made sure Faye always had a way to the big church with a neighbor or a family member.

After she graduated from high school, she went off to college at Troy State and received her degree in music and art. She eventually came back home and taught music and drama at Oakville High School for thirty years.

Ms. Faye never married. She always told people that her work and the kids she taught, along with her faith, made her life perfect, and she didn't need a man messing up the balance.

It was her twentieth year as music director for the church. Over time she had become one of the elders that people respected and admired.

During her tenure, she saw different pastors come and go, but in all the years as music director she had only ever missed one Sunday, and that was due to a Saturday night gallbladder attack that had her rushed to Mobile, AL for emergency surgery. She blamed the devil for the attack and gave God all the credit for her full recovery.

For several weeks in a row, Ms. Logan had noticed a visitor scratching on the church's side door before service. It was a fluffy, solid white cat she nicknamed Snowflake. She loved animals and was partial to cats, so the white feline couldn't have picked a better door to scratch.

The old music teacher asked several members of the church, but no one knew anything about the cat. The animal was so healthy and beautiful; it was apparent that someone was taking care of it.

Not wanting the poor thing to be hungry, she started bringing little treats from home to feed it at the side door. She even brought it inside a few times and gave it leftovers from the church kitchen. Better the cat gets it than it spoils, she would say to herself. The visiting feline and Ms. Logan made this a weekly routine that neither had any intention of breaking.

Tom walked out onto his back porch with a cup of coffee in one hand and Rex's yellow duck in the other. He had let the black Lab inside the house for a couple of hours the night before, and somehow the duck had gotten left behind.

"Rex," he called out. No sooner than his name was spoken than the young dog turned the corner of the house with both ears raised at attention and his nub wagging extra fast.

"Did you forget something last night?" Tom threw the yellow duck in the dog's direction.

The excited dog jumped and caught the stuffed toy then immediately started chewing on it, causing an annoying squeaking sound.

"We need to find a toy for you that doesn't make that noise," Tom complained.

The smell of coffee consumed the kitchen area. Lucky was stretched out in the center of Tom's bed, snoring.

While the java brewed, Tom came to two conclusions. The first was that he was starving, the second that he didn't seem to be in the mood to cook. That left only one option.

Fatbacks was a small, local, mom-and-pop diner that served breakfast, lunch, and supper but specialized in breakfast food, serving it until closing time. Along with the usual meats were the best homemade biscuits one could ask for, a breakfast casserole that could make a preacher cuss, and hot, homemade apple pies every morning.

Going to Fatbacks gave him an excuse to load Rex onto the back of the truck for a ride. The young Lab heard the house door open and immediately ran toward the front porch to see what the noise was about and who was making it.

The black Lab was almost big enough to jump on the tailgate by himself, but not quite. Still needing help, he sat at the rear of the truck and waited patiently for assistance.

"Maybe next weekend," Tom said as he lifted his dog onto the tailgate. Rex was growing so quickly that Tom knew it was just a matter of time before his Lab would be making that jump without him.

These trips to Fatbacks happened often enough that the young dog had figured out their timing. The fact that Tom ordinarily bought his two dogs a biscuit on these excursions helped the black Lab's memory.

The only thing Tom didn't like about Fatbacks was the gossip. The people who worked and hung out there in the mornings loved rumors, and they didn't always let the truth get in the way of a good story.

Who was getting a divorce? Who was cheating? Who was having money problems? Who was pregnant? Who was pregnant and getting a divorce? Who was cheating and having money problems? It was all discussed every morning around those old café-style tables. If someone graced the Fatbacks doorway, they could very well become part of that day's gossip.

Luckily there was a drive-through that Tom ordinarily took advantage of to avoid all the rumors and gossip that flowed inside the restaurant.

At the order window, he could see his Lab in the rearview mirror staring at the drive-through sign with a serious look as if he was about to place an order himself.

The lady on the other end of the speaker asked for Tom's order, then told him to drive up so the car behind him could place their order.

As he pulled up and put his truck in park, his cell phone started ringing. It was Hope.

"Hello," he answered.

"Hey, what are you doing?"

He paused for a second.

"Standing over this hot stove making breakfast," he complained.

"Really?" asked Hope.

"Yep, I just burned my finger."

Hope said nothing for a few seconds. "Well, I guess I better call the police then."

"What? Why?" Tom asked, sounding worried.

"Because someone has stolen your truck with your dog on the back and they are sitting in front of me in drive-through ordering breakfast."

"What are you talking about?" asked Tom.

"Goofy, look behind you," Hope said.

Tom turned and realized she had been behind him that whole time.

The waitress finally walked out with the food. "That'll be four seventy-five," she said cheerfully with a smile.

Tom handed her a five-dollar bill. "Keep the change," he added.

"Gee, sir, thanks, a whole twenty-five-cent tip," the waitress said sarcastically and walked off.

"Everyone's a comedian this morning," he said under his breath.

Plundering through the bag of food, he found the buttered biscuit that belonged to Rex and tossed it out the driver-side window into the truck bed. At first, the young Lab sat quietly and looked at it, but once the truck started moving, he reached down, grabbed the biscuit with his teeth, and finished it in three bites.

Driving home, he and Hope continued their conversation, and she asked him to go to church with her that morning. Now, the thought of going to church hadn't come close to entering Tom's mind, but Hope was very convincing.

"Okay, what time do you want me to pick you up?"

"Ten-thirty should work," Hope replied.

Tom knew he had no time to waste. He still needed to eat breakfast and bathe, and he wasn't sure if he had anything ironed and suitable. He forgot all about Rex as he drove home.

Back at home, he devoured his breakfast and jumped in the shower. With his teeth brushed and shower finished, he headed to his closet to find something to wear. It didn't take him long to find the same button-up white shirt and khaki pants that he'd worn last time he made it to Sunday service.

"This will do nicely," he said to himself.

Rex made his way to the front of the truck bed next to the cab and laid down. It wasn't unusual to be left alone on the truck for short periods, so the young Lab was content almost to the point of falling asleep. The dog loved to ride, and he had figured out that the back of the truck was the best place to make that happen.

Tom got ready for church so fast that he almost impressed himself. He still hadn't realized where Rex was. He looked in the bathroom mirror one more time.

"Okay, I'm ready." He grabbed his wallet, keys, and cell phone as he walked to the front door. Lucky followed behind him.

"You want to go outside, Lucky?" It was then that he remembered where Rex was.

He walked out on the front porch and called to Rex. The black Lab immediately popped his head up from the bed of the truck.

Rex never had a problem putting forth the effort to get on the truck. Getting off was an entirely different story. Someone usually had to use both hands and pull him to the edge of the tailgate, then lower him to the ground.

Tom was afraid his white shirt wouldn't fare well if he went through the normal process of getting Rex down. He looked at his watch; he didn't have time to iron another shirt.

He walked to the back of the truck and opened the tailgate. "Come on, buddy, jump down." The young dog went from a lying position to a sitting position but made no effort to get closer to the edge of the tailgate. Tapping the side of the truck, Tom tried again to convince his young Lab to jump down with no luck.

"Where's a sweet potato when you need one?"

Tom weighed the options: showing up at Hope's with a dirty shirt or taking Rex with him.

"Okay, boy, I guess you are going to church this morning."

He shut the tailgate, got into his truck and put the key in the ignition. Rex began to bark as if to hurry his owner.

Ten minutes later, they pulled into Hope's driveway. Hope stepped out of her house looking as pretty as Tom had ever seen her. He got out of his truck and walked around to the passenger side to open the door for her.

"You ready?" he asked.

Hope was too busy digging in her purse to answer him.

"What are you looking for?"

"Nothing in particular, just making sure I have everything I need."

Hope started toward the truck and saw Rex looking back at her from behind the back window. She stopped and looked at Tom. "You brought the dog?"

"Long story. I'll tell you on the way."

She climbed into the passenger seat. "So you're not afraid that he may jump off? What if he jumps off while we are in church?"

"He's not going to jump off. He loves the back of this truck. I have a hard time getting him off when we are at home."

Hope gave him a look of disapproval.

"Is that look something you do on purpose, or is it involuntary?"

"What look?" Hope replied, wearing a slight grin.

"That's what I thought," he answered.

Tom and Hope, along with Rex, pulled into the churchyard with about five minutes to spare.

"Man, there's a big crowd here today," Hope said, somewhat surprised.

Tom got out and opened the passenger-side door for his girl. He then walked to the back of the truck, where Rex was standing on the other side of the tailgate.

Rubbing the young black Lab's head, Tom leaned forward and whispered, "Please don't make me regret this." He grabbed Hope by the hand and pulled her closer. "You want to say a little prayer that Rex stays put?"

"Shut up," Hope answered.

Walking hand-in-hand toward the church's front doors, they saw Dr. Wright walking toward them.

"Good morning, Doc," Tom yelled as he extended his hand for a shake.

"Good to see you, Tom. I see you have your best half with you. Good morning, Ms. Hope. I believe you will be the prettiest lady at the service this morning," Dr. Wright said as he pulled his glasses down from his face.

Hope could only nod and smile. She didn't like anyone making a fuss over her, even for a good reason.

They were greeted by Ms. Logan as they walked inside.

"Good morning, Tom. Good morning, Hope. Now Hope, tell me how you managed to get this one to come this morning?" She pointed to Tom.

"It wasn't that hard."

"You know, Tom, we do this every Sunday. Same time, same place," Ms. Logan said as she handed him a church program.

"I know, Ms. Logan." Slightly uncomfortable, Tom pulled gently on Hope's arm. "We better find a place to sit. The service is about to start."

Tom surveyed the church congregation for a space big enough for him and Hope. He couldn't help but notice that he was looking at the same people sitting in the same places they had sat the last time he came.

Finally, he saw a spot at the end of the third pew from the front. Perfect, he thought as he tapped Hope's shoulder and pointed at the available space.

Pastor Sims had started preaching at a very young age. As a child, when the other boys he knew were out fishing, gigging frogs or tormenting girls in the neighborhood, he was reading his Bible.

He was baptized at the age of eight in a creek behind his family church. For as long as he could remember, all he had ever wanted to do was be a preacher. The young boy dreamed of being the leader of a church one day.

Growing up, he would stand in front of his mirror in his childhood bedroom and practice sermons. He delivered hundreds of messages into that mirror, practicing his cadence, movements and tone.

He became so good at it and felt so strongly about his faith and his calling that he became a pastor of a small Baptist church at the wise old age of seventeen. Later in life, he would say it was a good thing that he didn't know what he didn't know when he agreed to pastor that little church.

He led several churches during his career, some big, some small. He went into some churches knowing that they needed a shot of energy from him, and sometimes he found churches that allowed him to draw from its strength.

Even though he felt the members of his current church had been full of energy when he accepted the position of pastor three years ago, he now felt things had changed. The older church members didn't seem as excited and generous as they once were.

The congregation was losing younger members to graduations,

marriages, and job relocations. It had been over a year since a new member had joined. All these factors combined were beginning to concern Pastor Sims, so much so that he decided his sermon that Sunday would be different.

He felt that sometimes a pastor needed to find a higher gear. He was tired of the quiet, organized services, and he thought some of his members had become complacent.

The first thirty minutes of Rex's first trip to church were uneventful. He spent most of that time watching four large mockingbirds fly around and play.

Some occasionally landed and scratched for food. Rex never really chased birds, but they always fascinated him. The young Lab could easily spend an hour birdwatching with no intention of disturbing them.

The highlight of the first half hour was when a grass bird decided that one of the mockingbirds was too close to its nest and chased it away.

Rex's first and only experience with a cat had been with Vito. Because of that bad experience, Tom purposely kept Rex away from Vito. He knew that Hope's cat would not become any friendlier, and he also knew that his little Lab would not stay little for very long.

Even though Rex wasn't an aggressive dog, Tom feared he would end up hurting Hope's cat, even though it might not be his intention.

Rex hadn't lain eyes on a cat since the day Vito sent him underneath the porch, but that was about to change.

Snowflake had one bad habit. The cat enjoyed walking on vehicles. During the past month, every member of First Baptist had left church service with cat paw prints on their vehicle.

The white cat spotted Rex first, but this didn't stop him from starting his normal routine. The cat convinced himself that this Sunday would be no different than the previous ones.

He began with the pastor's Cadillac, walking back and forth across the hood until he was satisfied with himself. After it was covered with paw prints, he jumped over to the youth director's pickup.

The solid white cat enjoyed jumping from one car to the next without touching the ground. Next was Ms. Logan's Buick. No car was safe from having paw prints added to its design.

Rex was so engrossed with watching the mockingbirds that he missed the show Snowflake was putting on.

The feline had added his paw prints to just about every automobile in the churchyard that morning before making his way to Tom's truck.

There was no way Snowflake could know about Rex's history with cats. And maybe the cat had no reason to be afraid of dogs. Perhaps the dogs Snowflake had been around up to this point had been friendly. Whatever the reason, Snowflake didn't let the idea of a nearly grown black Lab being on the back of his next conquest bother him.

The curious cat approached Tom's truck and rubbed the side of its body against one of the front tires. He then walked behind the tire and used one of the steering arms as a backscratcher.

Rex had begun to notice Snowflake's scent. He stepped closer to the cab and hung his head over the body of the truck. By this time the young cat had made his way to one of the back tires and was cleaning his claws on its tread.

When the young Lab heard the noise from the cat's claws digging into the tire rubber, he quickly moved to the other side of the truck bed and looked down at the ground.

Both the white cat and the black Lab froze once they made eye contact. Rex recognized what he was seeing, and his first instinct was fear, but that fear quickly turned into curiosity with a dose of anger.

The white cat slowly took two steps backward to increase the distance between him and the strange dog. As Snowflake gave himself more of a head start, Rex let out a growl that confirmed the cat's idea of the dog's intentions.

The frightened cat quickly looked around for the closest tree, but there was none. There were cars everywhere but seeing a dog on the back of a truck for the first time made Snowflake think twice about using the top of a car as a safe place.

Rex lifted his front two legs onto the side of the truck body. He'd never jumped off from that position before but now found himself seriously considering it.

His urge to chase that cat was unbearable. All the black Lab knew was that the last time he saw one of those creatures, he had ended up hurt and scared to death. The young dog felt determined that would not happen again.

The stare-down continued as Rex sent a bark in the cat's direction. Snowflake was not moving a muscle but also not taking his eyes off the black Lab. The standoff lasted another minute or so until Rex finally couldn't hold himself back any longer.

Pulling with his front legs and pushing with his back legs, he climbed onto the truck's rear-side fender. For a half-second, he stood on top of it before he lunged toward Snowflake. He landed perfectly, his front feet hitting the ground first and his hind legs following close behind.

Snowflake didn't wait around to see if Rex stuck the landing. Seeing what was about to jump toward him, the young cat turned and ran in the opposite direction.

Mr. Harris was a chain smoker. Smoking was a habit he had picked up thirty-five years earlier in the Navy. He spent the majority of his service time on an aircraft carrier in the Pacific Ocean.

Smoking was a way to pass the time. According to Mr. Harris, if you were not on duty, you were smoking, eating, sleeping, or playing poker, and the latter made him want a cigarette.

One reason he continued the habit after he retired was it reminded him of some of the good experiences he had enjoyed in the Navy. It also reminded him of old friends he had made on that ship.

Mrs. Harris had spent the last five years trying to get Mr. Harris to attend a Sunday service. It wasn't that he had something against going to church. In fact, he had grown up in the First Baptist Church of Oakville and was baptized there at ten years old.

As a firm believer in God and the Bible, he watched church services on television while his wife was gone every Sunday morning. Mrs. Harris said that wasn't the same as being in church and hearing the message live, so she kept fussing at her husband until one day he broke down and promised her he would eventually go.

What kept Mr. Harris from going to church was fear. Fear that he would be unable to go without a cigarette long enough to make it through an hour-long service.

He tried everything to stop smoking. Gum patches, even a therapist, but nothing worked. It seemed the more he attempted to quit, the more he wanted a cigarette.

One day an idea came to him: if he could go twenty minutes without lighting up, and add five minutes to that time every day, then eventually he could make it to an hour. Wanting to make his wife happy, he felt this was a surefire way to do it.

Mr. Harris woke up that Sunday determined to take his wife to church. The day before, he had managed to go fifty minutes without lighting a cigarette. He was full of excitement; he wasn't sure the last time he had made it that long without smoking. The best part was it didn't seem that difficult. He noticed that once he passed the thirty-minute mark, it seemed to get easier.

When he told his wife about his plans that morning, she swelled up with joy. Fighting tears Mrs. Harris told him how proud she was and how excited it made her to know that she would be able to sit by her handsome husband during service that morning.

Preacher Sims took the handkerchief from his inside coat pocket and wiped the sweat from his forehead. He looked down at the watch he had placed on the pulpit to keep track of the time. It was eleven forty-five on the nose, and he had spent the last thirty minutes giving a sermon that he would later look back on and believe with all his heart that it was one of the best he had ever delivered.

The preacher's voice was louder than usual that morning. He moved around the pulpit with a different energy, and when he wanted an amen, he didn't wait for someone to volunteer one; he asked for it. The title of his sermon was "What does it take to be a starter on God's team?" He felt there were some toes in his church that needed to be stepped on, and today was the day to do the stepping.

Mrs. Harris always sat in the second row. She was somewhat hard of hearing, although she would never admit it. That Sunday, even she had no problem making out the preacher's words.

Mr. Harris heard everything loud and clear. In fact, he wondered if the preacher wasn't directing some of his message to him, since it had been so long since he had been to service.

He was the only person in the church that morning sweating more than Preacher Sims. When he had decided that making it through the whole service without a cigarette wouldn't be a problem, he had not accounted for a few realities.

He hadn't counted on someone ten feet away from him yelling for the better part of an hour. He had also forgotten how hot and stuffy that old church could be with a big crowd. Mr. Harris also had not considered having to be polite to a few church members who made it a point to remind him how long it had been since they last saw him.

But what made this really difficult for Mr. Harris was the fact that he could smell cigarette smoke. Someone that morning must have lit one up just before walking inside.

To make matters worse, that person smoked the same brand he did. He never thought he would have to sit there and smell the one thing he was trying to avoid during the whole service.

Mr. Harris looked at his watch. The urge to light one up was worsening by the second. He could easily smell a cigarette from thirty yards away, but the smell was coming from someone much closer than that.

He was experiencing withdrawals mixed with a minor panic attack. Everything seemed to become unbearable at once. The heat, the smell of smoke, and the noise combined to convince Mr. Harris that he needed to get out of there.

He remembered people coming in and out through a side door behind the pianist. That was his escape, he decided. He nudged his wife in the side, pointed to the door and told her he would meet her at the car. She assumed he needed to smoke and nodded her approval.

The poor fellow was so out of sorts that he didn't notice the side door not closing all the way when he tried to shut it behind him. The only thing on his mind was the cigarette he kept in his car above the sun visor for emergencies. The game of tag going on between Rex and Snowflake did not even get his attention.

That partially opened side door was a welcome sight for the white cat. Picking up speed, Snowflake headed toward the entrance. Ms. Logan had always been at that door when Snowflake needed her, so there was no reason for the young cat to think that this time would be any different.

Tom and Hope sat together and listened to every word Preacher Sims said. They both noticed a difference in his delivery of the message but agreed with the points he made.

As Preacher Sims finished his sermon, he asked everyone to bow their heads and close their eyes while he said a word of prayer. As Tom looked down and closed his eyes, he heard a bark.

Hope elbowed him in the rib cage. "Did you hear that?" she whispered, leaning toward him.

"I think you may have just broken one of my ribs," he answered. Tom recognized the bark and knew that it sounded too close for Rex to still be on the back of the truck.

Rex had never had this much fun chasing anything in his young life. He'd run after rabbits and squirrels before but never in a chase that lasted this long. Sometimes he tried to chase Lucky, but Lucky wasn't one to run from anything.

With his mouth wide open and his pink tongue almost dragging on the ground, Rex managed to stay within ten feet of the young cat.

The black Lab saw Snowflake disappear through the church's side door. Rex didn't know what was on the other side of that door, but this was the best chase he had ever been a part of, and he wasn't ready for it to end.

Just as Mr. Harris reached his car, he heard the commotion behind him and turned in time to see the white cat dart through the side door.

"Oh no," he said.

Everyone inside the church was sitting with bowed heads while Preacher Sims gave a very emotional final prayer of the day. Ms. Logan was sitting on the very first pew closest to the pianist, offering an occasional amen to encourage the preacher.

Somehow Snowflake ignored everyone inside the crowded church and instead made a beeline to Ms. Logan. The retired schoolteacher, unaware of what was coming her way, stood with eyes closed, calmly lost in the preacher's words until she felt four sets of claws digging firmly into the side of her arm. The young cat jumped toward the old woman and latched onto the first thing it landed on.

Mrs. Harris would later reluctantly admit that she had seen everything, which meant her eyes weren't closed during the final prayer.

Ms. Logan's scream as Snowflake dangled from her right arm didn't sound human. According to Mrs. Harris, once Snowflake saw Rex coming through the side door, he decided that being attached to Ms. Logan would not solve his current problem, so the young cat jumped down to the floor and onto the offering table before the pulpit.

Rex never slowed nor hesitated as he headed straight for the table. Both Ms. Logan and Mrs. Harris claimed they had never seen a dog move so quickly.

Snowflake was only on the offering table for a split second before he decided it wasn't tall enough. Quickly he jumped onto the pulpit, knocking over the microphone, which caused a terrible screeching sound that caught everyone off guard, including the cat.

He then jumped over a half partition into the choir area, found an open door that led into another room, and finally made his escape. Excited and confused, Rex ran back the way he had come, vanishing through the church's side door.

Tom and Hope were stunned, not believing what they had just witnessed. Tom wanted to run after his dog, but everything happened so quickly and unexpectedly that he just stood there.

"Whose cat?" Hope whispered.

As the preacher finished his prayer, Tom slowly looked around. It appeared that he and Hope, along with Ms. Logan and Mrs. Harris, were the only people who had seen what happened. Surprisingly, everyone else had kept their heads bowed and eyes closed.

He assumed the preacher had seen at least part of what happened but was grateful that he continued with the prayer. Tom also realized that the church was so full that the people in the back rows wouldn't have been able to see what happened anyway.

Preacher Sims never stopped praying, nor did he bother to open his eyes. He had heard Ms. Logan scream and the unnerving sound from the microphone when Snowflake knocked it over, just as everyone else had. He knew that something had happened around the offering table, but he didn't know what.

After his amen, he opened his eyes, not knowing what he might see. He looked around and saw that the only thing out of place was the microphone lying on its side on the pulpit.

Tom grabbed Hope by the hand, leaning toward her.

"We better go find Rex," he said.

Tom led Hope down the aisle as the congregation sang the last hymn of the day.

As they opened one of the big front doors, Tom looked toward his truck and saw Rex sitting in front of it.

"We may want to get him back on the truck before he sees that cat again," Hope suggested.

Tom agreed, so they picked up their pace toward Rex and started laughing before they reached the truck.

"This in no way, shape, or form is funny," Hope scolded.

"If you say so," Tom answered, still giggling.

Tom closed the tailgate behind his Lab.

"You crazy dog," he said as he scratched Rex under his chin.

Rex sat, looked Hope straight in the eyes, and started hassling.

"If I didn't know better, I'd say he was laughing," she said.

Before Tom could answer, Rex let out two quick barks.

Tom gave Hope the truck keys and ask her to crank the truck and start the air conditioner.

"Where are you going?" she asked.

He could see people walking out of the church. "I need to find Preacher Sims and Ms. Logan so I can apologize for what happened."

Tom saw Ms. Logan walking toward her car and decided to talk to her first while the preacher greeted everyone leaving the church.

"Ms. Logan," he yelled. She looked up and smiled at Tom. "I'm so sorry about my dog. I don't know what possessed him to jump off my truck. I don't know how he got inside the church. I never dreamed that something like that would happen, but I just wanted you to know I'm sorry."

"So the black dog belongs to you?" Ms. Logan asked.

"Yes ma'am, guilty as charged," Tom said with a smile.

"Do you have any idea who the cat belongs to?"

"I don't," he answered.

"Well, I guess it belongs to me now. I've been feeding that little rascal every Sunday for over a month. I should have taken it home before now. Don't worry about your dog. He was doing what dogs do when they see a strange cat."

When Tom made it to Preacher Sims, he was shaking the last hand of the day. Tom stuck his hand out for a shake and started to explain what happened.

When Tom finished apologizing, the preacher asked to meet Rex. Tom wasn't expecting to introduce Rex to the preacher, but he agreed.

The preacher leaned against the truck and rubbed Rex's head and shoulders for about two minutes without saying a word. Finally, he broke the silence, none too soon for Hope.

"Tom, as long as I'm preaching at this church, Rex will always be welcome here."

"Huh?" Tom said in disbelief.

"This beautiful dog is always welcome here. I can tell you are a little confused, so let me explain. After you and Hope walked out of the church, we had four people become saved and five people reaffirm their commitment to the Lord. Now, I would like to think that God used my preaching to make all that happen, but who's to say that the ruckus Rex caused today didn't play a role in it also? I've seen stranger things happen. I wouldn't change a thing about this morning, including Rex being here. Today wasn't a normal Sunday, and Rex for sure played a part in that," the old preacher said.

Tom smiled. "I'm glad you feel that way, Preacher. I'm happy that the morning worked out as it did. I'll see you next Sunday."

8

DEAD PIGS, COYOTES AND DIRT ROADS

It was a peaceful night. Calm to the point that the silence had begun to make a noticeable noise. Occasionally a car or truck would drive by and drown out the sound that the stillness seemed to be making.

Tom was sitting in one of the old rocking chairs on his front porch while Rex lay in front of him on point, waiting and watching for his human to make the next move. Tom had no intentions of making any sudden moves anytime soon; that old rocking chair felt good, and the more he rocked, the better it seemed to feel. Lucky was already in bed, asleep inside the house.

After a few more minutes of rocking, Tom realized he was in danger of nodding off, but the idea didn't bother him. Falling asleep, he felt Rex's nose nudging his knee. Realizing what was happening but ignoring it, he started to doze off again when he felt the same cold, wet nose rub against his hand that rested on the arm of the rocking chair.

Tom opened his eyes. There stood the black Lab, holding his yellow duck in his mouth, waiting for his human to give it a good throw. Rex tightened his grip on the toy so it would squeak. Tom smiled, grabbed the duck from the young Lab's mouth, and tossed it about twenty yards into the front yard.

He noticed a vehicle approaching that sounded like it was slowing down. Tom stopped rocking and started listening to the vehicle continue to slow down as it got closer.

Eventually, an old, black Chevy Nova turned into the driveway while blowing the horn. By this time Rex had forgotten about his duck and switched to guard-dog mode, running to the edge of the fence with his ears up, barking in the direction of the strange vehicle.

Nice car, Tom thought as he stood on the porch, waiting to see whom it belonged to. The driver's door opened, and Mike jumped out of the car looking happy and proud.

"Hey man, how do you like it?" he asked as he walked toward the front gate.

Tom and Mike had been friends for most of their lives. They had met in kindergarten, remained close throughout elementary school and junior high, and graduated high school together.

After high school, the two slowly drifted apart but occasionally planned fishing trips together. Mike was a little rough around the edges, always jumping between jobs and relationships, never really wanting to be tied down by anyone or anything.

He eventually received his CDL to become a truck driver. By this time, he'd spent the last five years jumping from one trucking company to the next.

"A truck driver can always find a job," he bragged.

Tom, somewhat in shock, didn't know what to say. He had never seen Mike own anything other than an old, beat-up Nissan pickup.

"Well, say something," Mike scolded.

Tom stepped off the porch to get a closer look at the Nova.

"That is an awesome-looking car."

"Thanks. I spent an hour trying to find something wrong with it before I bought it, but it's perfect—new paint job, new interior, new chrome wheels, and the tires are practically new. Did you notice how the motor sounded when I pulled up?"

Tom, still in disbelief, managed to answer that question faster. "Yes, the motor sounds great. How did you end up buying it?"

"Well, I signed on to drive with a new trucking company a few days ago, and I'm getting an four-thousand-dollar sign-on bonus. I received two of it today; I'll get the rest on my one-year anniversary. So anyway, I went to Montgomery today to buy some things I needed to go out over the road, and something told me to go the back way up highway thirty-one, so I did, and I ran up on this car for sale. The guy I bought it from just found out his wife is having triplets and I think he was in a state of panic, because he sold me this car for a crazy low price, so low that I couldn't pass it up."

While Mike continued telling Tom about the car, Rex opened the latch on the front gate with his nose and decided to give the old Nova an inspection of his own. Around thirty seconds into it, the black Lab commenced to lifting his leg and giving each of those shiny wheels a baptism. The way Rex saw it, the car now belonged to him. Fortunately, neither Tom nor Mike noticed the extra attention that the young dog was giving Mike's new toy.

"Let's go for a ride," Mike said with excitement.

"I don't know; it's getting late."

"Come on, it's Friday night, and I'm guessing since you are sitting here alone with your dog, your schedule must be pretty open."

Tom wished he could argue, but Mike was right. Since Hope had begun helping her sick aunt, his Friday and Saturday nights left a lot to be desired.

"Jump in, let's go," Mike said.

Tom couldn't think of a good reason not to. "Okay, let me put Rex back in the yard."

"Don't worry, I have a blanket in the trunk. I'll spread it over the backseat, and he can come with us. I've already let my beagle ride back there."

Mike had always been a bigger dog person than Tom.

With the backseat covered, Rex planted himself in the center of the seat as if he needed to see the view of the road. Mike paused a second to buckle his seatbelt. Tom followed his lead and buckled himself in as the trio pulled out of the driveway.

"I can't believe how smooth this old car rides," Tom bragged. Mike just smiled and nodded as he drove down the old country road.

Both guys remembered a simpler time when they were younger and rode those country highways and dirt roads around Oakville for entertainment.

Rex, on the other hand, was not being entertained. Five minutes of watching the view between Tom and Mike was all it took to make the young Lab crave sleep, so that's what he did. That old backseat made a good dog bed, and Rex took advantage of it.

"I think your dog is snoring back there."

Tom didn't answer; he was enjoying the old car's sound and the smooth ride it offered.

Thirty minutes became an hour, and the first hour quickly became hour number two as the two guys just rode and talked as if they were teenagers again.

"We should do this more often," Mike suggested as he pulled down another dirt road to explore. Tom agreed with a nod and a smile.

Meanwhile, Rex had finished his nap and was leaning his head out of the backseat window. His bright pink tongue blew toward the back of his head from the cool wind rushing alongside the car. Every so often, he let out what sounded like a bark of approval as he enjoyed pressing his face against the fresh night air.

As they came to the end of another dirt road, Mike noticed headlights coming from his left and decided to wait and let it pass. He looked over in Tom's direction and couldn't believe what he was seeing.

"Dude, look over there," Mike said, pointing toward the passenger-side window. Tom quickly turned his head to see what had his chauffeur's attention and couldn't believe what he saw.

"Pigs?" Tom blurted out before he even fully realized what he had seen.

"There are three of them, and they are huge!" Mike said in disbelief.

"How do three farm-raised pigs end up here?"

"Three fat farm-raised pigs," Mike added.

By this time, the vehicle coming in their direction was only a few hundred yards away. Tom noticed that one of the pigs was getting dangerously close to the edge of the road.

"Hey pig, come here," he yelled as if the pig understood human.

The distracted hog took two more steps onto the roadway, putting it directly in the path of the oncoming box truck flying toward it.

"That truck isn't slowing down. This is going to get ugly," Mike predicted.

As if the truck driver heard Mike's warning, the truck began to quickly slow down and veer off to the right of the pig but was unable to avoid hitting it.

The fat hog blurted out a screech that sent his two companions running across the road into the woods. Mike and Tom sat in the old black Nova, neither believing what they had just seen as they watched the truck's taillights dim in the distance.

Finally, after about ten seconds of silence, Rex, who had not taken his eyes off the three pigs since he first noticed them, began to bark and whimper, letting Tom know he wanted out of the car.

"Oh no, Rex, the last thing I need is for you to get lost chasing those other two hogs deeper into the woods," Tom said. "Hell, with my luck you would find a baby wolf and bring it back with you."

"I think we just witnessed a hit-and-run," Mike joked.

Before Tom had time to reply, Mike unbuckled his seat belt and opened the door.

"Where are you going?"

"To get that pig. That's a lot of fresh ham lying in the road."

"You are joking, right?" he asked, even though he knew Mike was serious as a stroke.

As Tom watched Mike drag the pig toward the car, he was reminded why he had decided a long time ago to stop hanging around with his childhood friend so much.

Rex let out another bark followed by a pitiful noise that sounded like a combination of a whimper and a cry. He started pacing back and forth in the backseat.

"What's wrong with you, boy?" Tom asked.

Something was upsetting Rex, and this wasn't the run-of-the-mill flustered that Tom sometimes saw when Rex wanted attention or extra food in his bowl. No, Tom knew, this was different.

"Okay, let's get you out of this car. Maybe that will calm you down." Tom opened the door, stood, pulled his belt off and looped it underneath Rex's collar. "Okay, it's not a leash, but it will keep you from running off."

Tom barely got the car door halfway open before Rex hit the ground on all fours and started pulling him toward the edge of the road. He pulled back on his belt to stop Rex's progress. The black Lab sat and let out three quick barks toward the other side of the road. Tom assumed the Lab was pulling him that way because that was the direction the pigs had run.

Mike was more than halfway back to the car, pulling the pig by his hind feet when he looked up to asked Tom for some help. Before he could speak, he saw four sets of eyes shining from the other side of the road, staring back at him.

"Tom," Mike yelled. "Get Rex back in the car and help me get this pig in the trunk." As soon as Mike finished the sentence, he pointed toward the road. By that time, they could see that the four sets of eyes Mike saw belonged to a pack of coyotes that also had plans for the dead pig.

They now knew that it wasn't the idea of the pigs getting away but the four coyotes that had Rex so restless. Tom pulled on the black

Lab's collar, but Rex wouldn't move as he sat there and watched the four dog-like animals.

Tom jerked on Rex's collar once more. "Come on, let's go," he ordered, raising his voice with each syllable. Rex slowly stood and growled as he took two steps backward, never taking his eyes off the four coyotes.

As they moved closer to the old Nova, Tom noticed that Rex made sure to stay between him and the coyotes. Slowly but surely, they both made it to the car. Once Rex was inside, Tom shut the door and ran toward Mike to help with the pig.

On the count of three, they hoisted the pig and dropped him inside the trunk. By this time, all four coyotes were walking in big circles around the car as if deciding which one would attack first. Rex was barking nonstop inside the car, encouraging Tom and Mike.

"Okay, let's get out of here," Tom yelled. They wasted no time getting into the old Nova and shutting the doors.

"Now would be an awful time for this old car not to start," Mike said with a chuckle.

"Why would you even say that right now?" Tom complained as he rolled up the window.

The old Chevy eliminated all the suspense by cranking up on the first turn of the key.

"I knew I liked this car for some reason," Tom said.

Mike threw the old Nova in drive and punched the gas.

Rex turned and looked out the back windshield and barked two more times, warning the wild dogs not to follow them.

"Dead pigs, coyotes, and dark, abandoned dirt roads, all rolled up into one relaxing drive. That's the making of a pretty intense nightmare I can now have one night," Tom joked as he buckled his seatbelt again.

"So does that mean you are ready to go home?" Mike asked.

"Yep, I think we have had enough excitement for one trip."

Mike turned down another dirt-covered road that would take them to Tom's house. The black Lab decided to lie down in the back seat and catch another nap. It turned out to be an exciting trip for Rex as well, considering he had seen his first coyote and his first pig all in the same night.

Tom was also thinking about a nap when he heard a noise from the back of the car. "Did you hear that?" he asked Mike.

"Yeah, it was Rex." The noise happened again, but this time it was louder. It sounded like something beating against the back of the Nova.

"That's not Rex," Tom said, some concern in his voice.

Mike slowed the car to see if he could hear the sound more clearly.

"There it is again," Mike announced, putting both hands on the steering wheel. "The car is driving fine. It's not a bad tire."

"It's coming from the trunk, and I think it's the pig."

"It's what?" Mike asked.

"It's the pig," Tom repeated.

"Tom, the pig is dead!"

"Well maybe you need to stop the car, and one of us can open the trunk and remind him of that."

The noise was getting louder and Rex, interrupted from his nap, was now pacing back and forth sniffing the backseat. He knew there was something on the other side that shouldn't be there.

"So you think the pig was playing possum?" Mike asked.

"I don't know, but the sound is coming from the trunk, and the pig is the only thing inside the trunk."

When Mike found a safe place to pull over, the guys made their way to the back of the car. It became clear by the commotion inside the trunk that the pig was very much alive and unhappy with its current situation.

"That hog is pissed, so what are we going to do?" Mike asked.

"We? Him being inside that truck was your idea. Open the trunk, let the pig out, and let's go home," Tom scolded.

Mike didn't want to let the pig go, but he couldn't think of a better idea. So he unlocked the trunk door but held it down while he stepped to the side of the car.

Once he thought he was in a safe place, he slowly lifted the door enough that the light came on inside the trunk. There he was, the pig that was dead fifteen minutes ago now looking back at his captor wearing what almost looked like a grin. Mike was thinking about all the ham sandwiches he could make at the pig's expense.

"Porky, you have been one lucky hog tonight," Mike said as he opened the door all the way. The pig needed no encouragement; the second there was enough of an opening, he darted out of the trunk and ran into the woods.

Mike shut the door and got back in the car. "Oh well, win some, lose some," he said.

Tom looked at Mike and smiled, then pointed to his watch. Neither said a word; they were both ready to call it a night.

9

WITH ADVENTURE COMES RISK

Sitting in the front yard, Rex watched Lucky make his final rounds inside the fence's perimeter. This was the house dog's last venture outside before going to bed, so he was making the most of it, sniffing and marking every few steps. It was a show that the black Lab saw his old buddy perform every night, so he wasn't very interested in getting up and joining in.

Rex was bored, that night and the day it followed was uneventful. No rides on the back of the truck, no walks to the pond and no new discoveries to distract him. Since Luck was making his last walk of the night, the young Lab knew that the quiet that covered the yard would become even more noticeable once the house was silent.

Tom eventually opened the front door and walked out onto the porch. He looked in Rex's direction as he leaned over the back of one of the old rocking chairs.

"Whatcha doing, boy?" Tom asked, not expecting Rex to move or respond. He then called out to Lucky.

The old lap dog trotted from around the side of the house, scampered up the front steps and continued through the front door. He knew a cozy bed awaited him inside.

Rex, not realizing what a cozy bed was, lay on the damp grass and watched as one by one all the house lights disappeared, making the full moon stand out even more.

This was the Lab's least favorite time of day. No Tom or Lucky. No one to talk to him or throw his toy duck. No squirrels chasing one another up and down the oaks. No birds playing in the yard. Even the gas station next door was dark. To the Lab, it seemed he was the only animal on the hill not asleep.

After a few minutes, Rex got up and walked over to his water bowl for a drink before his first nap of the evening. The fresh water tasted good as he lapped it up with his tongue. With a dripping wet snout, he walked toward the front yard to his favorite napping place.

The corner under the porch wasn't just a good hiding place. As far as Rex was concerned, it was also the best place on the whole property for a good nap. It was cool in the summer and warm in the winter. The dirt there was always soft, and there was a shallow hole that fit his body perfectly. Not to mention the young Lab just felt safe there.

Once settled, it wasn't long before Rex was dreaming just as hard as the rest of the animals on the property. His back legs twitched every so often as he tried to catch the rabbit he chased in his sleep. The chase became so realistic that he let out a few soft barks as he lay there.

Patch disliked the boredom of the nightlife around his house just as much as Rex did his. The difference was he wasn't trapped behind a security fence. Patch loved Fred, but when his master turned in at night, the half-wild dog didn't see the need to hang around Fred's house with Marcy.

Tom's plan for Fred to fall in love with Patch as he bottle-fed the abandoned puppy had worked exactly as hoped. Neither of the men ever mentioned the deal made the day Tom had brought the starved animal to him. Fred cared for the lost animal like an infant, allowing it to grow into a strong, handsome dog.

If Tom or Fred visited one another, that meant Rex and Patch got to visit one another also. The half-wild puppy and the young black Lab ran together, wrestled together, and hunted for mischief together. The two dogs were inseparable when they were on the same property at the same time.

Ten month old Patch was a mixture of breeds, although no one agreed on the recipe. Fred was convinced that the one-eyed dog was part wolf with some border collie. Dr. Wright believed he was husky and Australian shepherd mixed. Tom guessed that he was a combination of Australian shepherd husky and border collie. All three agreed that Patch was a beautiful, unique-looking animal.

Tonight, sleep came easy for Rex. So easy, in fact, that he now had a raccoon treed up an oak as he lay twitching his front legs. Just as it looked like the little monster would jump to the ground and make a run for it, something startled Rex. He opened one eye. He lay still for a moment, then he heard a noise from the front gate.

The sleepy black Lab suddenly became a guard dog as he crawled out from under the porch. He looked toward the front gate. Through the darkness, he saw Patch standing on the other side of the fence. He immediately recognized him, so he relaxed and sent a half-hearted bark in his friend's direction as he sat and shook some dust off his coat.

Ordinarily, Rex would have been more excited to see the one-eyed dog, but he had just awakened from a deep sleep and been interrupted from a dream in which he was about to catch his first raccoon.

Most nights, Patch's visits began and ended the same way, with both dogs barking and touching noses through a locked gate. They would become bored, and eventually Patch would continue his adventure elsewhere, but tonight would be different.

As Rex sat there trying to wake up, he noticed that the latch on the front gate looked different. He stood and walked toward the fence to investigate, but before he could reach the gate, Patch used his nose to lift the latch upward, dropping the lock onto the ground.

Neither dog could have realized that earlier that night, Tom had opened the gate on the way to his truck. When he came back in, he hung the lock over the side of the latch instead of locking it, thinking he would make the same trip again. The second trip never happened, so the gate was never locked.

Both dogs stood there and looked at one another in silence. This had never happened before. Neither had expected the door to open, so neither knew what to do next. Finally, Patch walked through the gate and went straight for Rex's water bowl. The young Lab sat and watched the half-wild dog drink half of his water.

After the water break was over, both dogs played a game of keep-away with the yellow duck in Tom's front yard. The game ended when Rex accidentally slung the duck toward the front porch into one of the rocking chairs.

A while later, Patch became restless and ran outside the fence, looking back at Rex in hopes that the black Lab would follow. The Lab hesitated; he had never been outside the gate after dark. The one-eyed dog began to whimper, encouraging his friend to chase him.

Eventually, the temptation became more than the young Lab could ignore. Not ready for the night to end and not wanting to lose sight of his partner, he let out a bark to find his courage, then darted through the front gate behind his restless friend. Seeing that Rex was going to follow, Patch turned and headed across the road into the woods.

Keeping up with the large, athletic dog wasn't easy, but Rex enjoyed every second of it. The playful Lab hadn't enjoyed himself this much since he chased that cat into the church.

They climbed hills, ran through creeks, and explored a cave. They played in pastures and discovered a pond new to both of them.

Patch spent most nights hunting for excitement, so he knew all the best places to visit, and he intended to prove it to the black Lab.

Rex had always been content running in and exploring Tom's property and never roaming far from it. He didn't realize there were animals nearby waiting to be discovered. On this night he saw a cow for the first time. He also discovered turkeys that night. The two dogs also met a horse, which excited Rex to no end.

The young Lab became overloaded with new animals, new sights, and new smells. But not every new experience on this night would be a good one. Rex would learn that not all animals were friendly like the horses he had just met or cowardly like the squirrels back home.

When Patch began leading him back home through a different set of woods and pastures, the black Lab didn't realize it. Their adventure was in its fourth hour, and the one-eyed dog's internal clock was telling him that he needed to be heading home soon himself.

With about a mile through the woods left before Rex's adventure would end, they came across a pasture full of sheep. Loaded with curiosity, the young Lab stopped suddenly and stared at the creatures. Since it was his first experience seeing the cotton-like animals, he couldn't help but be amazed. Most were lying down but awake, while a few stood as if they were guarding the rest.

The still silence lasted for a minute or so until Patch let out a bark that sounded to Rex like a warning of sorts. The bark broke him out of his trance caused by the peaceful sheep. He looked around, searching for his half-wild companion.

Before the black Lab could find Patch, another bark sounded from a group of sheep directly in front of him. Rex walked through and around the fluffy white creatures eager to see his friend. He finally made it to where Patch was standing and immediately saw what had caused the warning barks.

The one-eyed dog was sniffing a blood-soaked area on the ground. Rex recognized the scent of blood from whenever Tom cleaned fish, although he had never seen this much of it in one place. He also realized from the smell that this wasn't fish blood.

The black Lab dropped his nose to the ground and followed a blood trail for about twenty yards toward the tree line on the other end of the pasture. The tracks were less than an hour old.

Patch caught up with Rex and stood beside him, both dogs looking toward the woodline where the trail disappeared. The half-wild dog not only sensed danger, but also smelled it. He didn't like what he was seeing or smelling, and it made him uneasy.

Within a minute, both dogs heard yelps and barks from the direction of the tree line. The noises grew louder and more intense by the second. The sheep became restless and started bleating loudly.

The dogs had no way of knowing that their adventure had led them into a kill zone. The blood belonged to a sheep that was the latest victim of a pack of coyotes hanging out that night in the woods beside the pasture. Using the full moon as a nightlight, the wild animals had killed the defenseless creature, then dragged it into the trees and fed off it. What made matters worse was the fact that the coyotes were still hungry and returning to the kill zone for more food.

There were six members in the pack, so the one kill earlier that night didn't go very far. Sheep were easy targets because they were not very fast and didn't put up much of a fight.

One by one, each coyote stepped out from the cover of the woodline into the moonlight, hassling with their white teeth shining like pearls. Two of them still had blood on their chest from the first kill that night—all looked forward to another easy meal before sunrise.

Patch understood what the coyotes wanted. This wasn't his first time running across this pack. While he didn't consider them friends, he had no desire to make enemies of them that night. The one-eyed canine wasn't going to join in on the next kill, but he didn't intend to stop it either. Rex, on the other hand, felt differently.

About halfway between the dogs and the coyotes lay a baby sheep that had wandered away from the group. It stood up from a nap and began to call out for its mom. Rex and the coyotes heard the lamb at the same time, but the black Lab's intentions were far different from those of the group of hungry dogs.

The lamb's cry for help was the only sound from the pasture, making it an even bigger target. Rex stood and watched as the two bloodstained coyotes got up and started walking toward what they thought would be an easy kill. Showing no fear, the young Lab trotted over to the desperate lamb and positioned himself between it and the wild dogs.

Realizing that getting the next meal may be more complicated than they first thought, the rest of the pack stood, lowered their heads, and began to jog toward the new kill zone. The yelps and barks became louder and more intense. The coyotes all agreed that the crying lamb would be their next victim even if they all needed to join the hunt to make it happen.

This wasn't a fight he would have picked, but understanding that the numbers didn't favor his partner, Patch began to run toward Rex and the lamb. If the one-eyed dog wasn't half-wolf, it wasn't because he lacked the wild animal's size, agility, or speed. Once at Rex's side, Patch let out two barks toward the gang of wild dogs, letting them know that he would have to be dealt with also.

Rex's fighting experience came from the arguments and scraps between him and Patch growing up together. Although Patch was younger than Rex, he eventually outgrew the black Lab, which sometimes created a problem when Rex's plans didn't match his. Like brothers, sometimes those battles became serious, but neither dog meant to hurt the other. Those disagreements and fights between the two served as good training for what was about to happen.

Within seconds, all six coyotes were circling the new kill zone that Rex, Patch and the baby lamb now found themselves trapped inside. The bobtailed Lab and the one-eyed dog stood with their back ends touching one another, gnashing their teeth and barking loudly and quickly to convince the predators that a second meal would be too much trouble.

Feeling there was safety in numbers, the coyotes continued to close in for the kill. Gradually each hunter got a little closer to their victims as they completed circles around their prey. One of the blood-stained coyotes decided to make a move for the lamb, but his attempt only yielded him a cut on his snout from one of Rex's fangs.

Seeing the wild dog rejected only excited the rest of the pack even more. With the full moon encouraging the hungry dogs, the yelps and barks became louder, echoing throughout the pasture.

A second coyote decided it was his turn to try for the lamb but was pushed to the dirt by one of Patch's big paws without much trouble. Knowing another attack was on its way, the one-eyed dog quickly let up his attacker and returned his attention to the pack. This coyote merry-go-round lasted for several minutes with each wild dog trying more than once to grab the baby lamb with no success.

After a while, the coyotes realized their advantage in numbers and began to strike in unison. Instead of one at a time, they commenced attacking in pairs. When that didn't work, the pack sent three dogs in at a time. Although still managing to keep the baby lamb safe, Rex and Patch were beginning to lose track of where the wild dogs were coming from.

The one-eyed dog's frustration turned into anger as he grabbed one of the attacking coyotes by the back of the neck, picked him up off the ground and slung him back into the pack of hunters. Rex felt that same anger, clutching one of the attackers by the throat and slamming it to the ground. Even if a fight wasn't what the wild dogs had been looking for, a fight was what they got.

While both dogs held their own against the coyotes, Rex started to show signs of fatigue. Patch was bigger, faster, and stronger, so he was holding up better.

The baby lamb continued to cry for help as both of its protectors now stood over it, shielding it from the attacks that were getting closer to succeeding.

The coyotes' plan of wearing down their adversaries without putting themselves in a lot of danger was working nicely. Never mind that the two dogs managed to keep the upper hand. There was no way Rex and Patch could keep up with the pace of the attacks for much longer. Eventually, the two dogs would have to make a decision: let the pack have the lamb or possibly become prey themselves.

Suddenly, the coyotes stopped in their tracks. Not making a noise, the pack stood and looked at one another as if they were confused. The lamb also stopped crying. Silence fell on the pasture with the only sound being a lonely cricket chirping.

The coyotes had heard and smelled something that made them forget about eating. Rex and Patch also noticed a different scent. No longer circling their food, the wild dogs huddled up and started to make their way back to the wood line for protection. They recognized the odor from the darkness of the pasture and decided it would be easier to find a meal elsewhere. The hunters now felt like the hunted, and they could not get back into the woods fast enough.

Rex watched as the wild dogs jogged back in the direction they had come from. Patch heard a noise behind him and turned to investigate.

Out of nowhere walked three large sheepdogs that protected that pasture and the sheep in it. The baby lamb's cry for help had finally brought reinforcements, and not a moment too soon. From a distance, those dogs looked like sheep themselves, only larger and with no reason to fear coyotes.

No longer a kill zone, the area began to fill up with sheep again, with some even taking the time to play. With their thick, white, wool-like coats, the sheepdogs stood in silence, studying Rex and Patch. Even though they meant the sheep no harm, the two visitors realized that those sheepdogs didn't want them in their pasture. Slowly they backed away from the baby lamb and turned toward Rex's house to finish their trip.

▲ ▲ ▲

Victor Evans didn't realize he was the town drunk, which was a good thing because if he had known, he would have had another reason to pick up a bottle. In his late fifties, he was forty pounds overweight, with white hair retreating to the back of his neck.

If you lived in Oakville and you told someone you saw Mr. Evans, they wouldn't bother to ask if he was drunk because they already knew the answer. But in Victor's mind, he was still the clean-cut, sober man who had served two terms as mayor of Oakville some twenty years earlier—always with a coat, tie, and smile, trying to shake the hands of townspeople as he walked the downtown streets.

The truth, which Mr. Evans tried his best to avoid, was that a failed business, two divorces and a landslide election that didn't go his way had taken their toll on the once-respected mayor, so much so that his only escape was at the bottom of a whiskey bottle.

On that particular night, while Rex and Patch were saving a lamb from a pack of hungry coyotes, Victor was being thrown out of a poker game because he was too impaired to recognize his hand.

"I've been escorted out of better dumps than this," he yelled as he staggered to his car.

To his credit, Victor had a spotless driving record. No DUIs, no accidents, not even a parking ticket. When he got behind the wheel of a car, he was as steady and careful as a preacher driving in a church parking lot on Sunday morning. Little did he know that his perfect driving record would take a hit that night.

With only one more highway to cross before he reached home, Rex's journey was reaching the end. It was a long night for both dogs, but the bobtailed dog wasn't used to the all-nighters that Patch enjoyed. He was one tired and thirsty black Lab, and his body was making him aware of it.

The two dogs walked out of a wooded area at one corner of a four-way stop about half a mile from Tom's house. Rex could not only see the security lights from his yard but also smell the familiar scents of home.

Patch nudged the young Lab's face with his nose and let out a bark as if to say "See you later," then turned in the opposite direction and commenced jogging home.

This wasn't the first time Rex had been this tired or this thirsty, but this was the first time he experienced both at the same time. The only two things he could think about as he walked toward home were the water waiting for him in his bowl and his comfortable, safe spot under the front porch.

After his gambling ended prematurely, Mr. Evans decided he would ride around and finish off a bottle of whiskey he had borrowed off the poker table just before being escorted outside. Holding his bottle in one hand and fighting the radio with his other, Victor controlled the steering wheel of his old Cadillac with his knees.

By the time he reached the four-way stop that the dogs had just left, the car radio and whiskey were winning the battle for his attention, with the road in front of him a distant third.

Unable to find a song he liked, Mr. Evans became angry and ran through the stop sign without slowing down. Not realizing how fortunate he was, he continued down the road while making up new cuss words to describe his feelings about the car radio.

Rex saw lights coming toward him but paid them little attention; noise from traffic was a common occurrence to him. Still thinking about home, he continued walking on the grass along the side of the highway.

While Mr. Evans unknowingly closed the distance between him and the exhausted dog, his car swerved twice into the opposite lane and once onto the grass, almost going into the ditch. Driving mostly with his knees, he was unaware of how close he came to losing control of his Cadillac.

With only a few hundred yards separating him and his water bowl, Rex stopped to cross the highway between him and the entrance leading to Tom's house. He looked both ways and saw the lights from the car that he heard getting closer by the second. The young Lab stood by the road and patiently waited for the car to pass so he could finish the last steps of his exciting night.

Unaware that a dog was giving him the right of way, Victor Evans set his bottle of spirits on the dashboard as he reached into his shirt and grabbed a fresh cigarette. The vibration from the road and a slight jerk of the steering wheel caused the bottle to tilt forward, falling onto the floor of the passenger side and splashing whiskey into the front seat.

His attention now solely on the whiskey, Mr. Evans quickly leaned down to grab his bottle of courage before all of it emptied onto the floorboard. With one hand holding his smoke and the other reaching for his spirits, his knee steered the car off the road into the grass. He felt the front right wheel wobble as he heard a thud and then a terrible howl. Acting on his first instinct, he slammed on the brakes and took hold of the steering wheel, this time with both hands.

"I just hit something," he said, guiding the car off the road. "Oh my God, what if it was somebody?" he asked himself. The answer to that question came in a hurry when he heard another awful howl along with a whine.

"That's a dog," he mumbled, continuing to talk to himself. The relief that Mr. Evans felt covered him like a blanket as he realized it was an animal and not a human. Becoming soberer each time he blinked his eyes, he sat there and took deep breaths, trying to calm himself.

Feeling his heart rate slow down, he started to wonder whose dog he had run over. He also thought he might be able to help the poor animal. Mr. Evans wasn't sober much, but he wasn't heartless either. He opened his door, stood, and steadied himself by holding onto the seat.

Pain and shock covered Rex's body as he lay on the ground with no idea what had just happened or how he ended up there. The blow to his head from the Cadillac's front bumper had taken his memory of the last few minutes away. The last thing he remembered was Patch nudging him at the four-way stop.

With dirt in his mouth and eyes, the injured Lab couldn't feel one of his legs. His head pounded and everything was blurry, but he could see red lights in front of him and a human standing above him. He hoped it was Tom.

A tear rolled down Mr. Evans' face as he stood there, looking at the scarred and broken dog. Although not entirely sober, he was coherent enough to realize that the injured Lab's hind leg wasn't supposed to bend that way. He also understood that the young dog was lying there on the ground, trembling with fear, because he had swerved off the road and hit him.

Now on his knees, Mr. Evans reached for Rex's collar to see if he had an identification tag.

"Who do you belong to?" he asked, lifting Rex's head off the ground to get a closer look.

While searching for a tag, it dawned on him that he recognized the animal.

"You belong to Tom. Why wasn't you behind that fence? You are always behind the fence," he said, fighting back tears.

By now, the old drunk had remembered the young dog as the Lab he always saw at Tom's house. The relief he had felt a few minutes earlier had all but disappeared, replaced by sorrow for not paying more attention to the road.

Rex, still looking for Tom while realizing his pain was worsening, listened as the human continued the conversation with himself.

"It was an accident; I didn't mean to do it—that damn whiskey bottle. What if this had been a kid?"

Mr. Evans' discussion continued for a few more minutes.

"I'm going to get you home, but you have to promise not to bite me," the old man said, attempting to negotiate.

Still unsure how he had ended up there, Rex listened to everything the human said, hoping his pain would go away. The young Lab could smell the strong odor of whiskey escaping from Mr. Evans' body but had no idea what it was.

Feeling more sober than he had in ages, the old drunk brought a blanket back from his car and carefully placed it under Rex's battered body. Once satisfied, the old man began to pull both the cover and the black Lab toward his Cadillac.

"Okay, you be still while I do the work here," he said, straining to keep his grip as he pulled.

At the car, he opened the door to the backseat, then looked down to once again ask the black Lab not to bite him.

"I couldn't blame you if you did, but I'd surely appreciate it if you didn't," he added.

Holding two corners in each hand, Mr. Evans used the blanket to lift his victim off the ground and into the back seat of his Cadillac. The black Lab let out a yelp as he hit the seat.

"Okay, that wasn't as hard as I thought it might be," Victor announced proudly. "Let's get you behind that fence."

Head throbbing and afraid to move, Rex lay as still as he could while the car cranked up. The young dog was unaware that he was so close to home. Within seconds, he noticed the car coming to a stop.

With the shock and fear from the accident subsiding, which allowed the buzz from the whiskey to return, Mr. Evans climbed out of the Cadillac, opened the back door and reached for the four corners of the blanket.

"Home sweet home," he yelled, not considering the young Lab's pain or the fact that he was in someone else's yard before daylight.

"Well, no wonder you were out by the road; the gate is open. Tom needs to be more careful," the old drunk complained.

By a stroke of good fortune, Victor managed to carry Rex inside the fence without dropping him.

Inside the yard, he eased Rex to the ground, dropped to his knees, and began to talk to the injured dog as if he were speaking to an old friend.

"There's no reason to wake Tom up this early. I'm going to put you in the front yard here so he can find you when he gets up. Honestly, that leg looks terrible, but Dr. Wright should be able to have you back up and playing in no time. Thank you for not biting me even though you should have. Oh, I also need that blanket back. And I am so sorry that I ran you over."

After he finished his intoxicated rambling, the old man stood and proceeded to stagger to the car, carrying his bloody blanket and locking the gate behind him.

With cuts and wounds scattered over his body, Rex lay in the front yard, afraid to make a sound. Even with the pain and confusion clouding his brain, Rex was relieved to be home.

Lying there tasting dirt and blood, he had never remembered being so thirsty. He knew where his water bowl was, but he was also afraid to make a decision, even one as simple as killing his thirst.

Raising his body into a sitting position, he noticed his broken leg for the first time as it fell awkwardly away from the rest of his body. The black Lab figured out quickly that he no longer controlled that leg, so he managed to stand using his front two legs and his one good back leg.

For the first time, he felt pain from the broken hind leg as it dangled clumsily from his hip, allowing his foot to drag on the ground. He stood there for some time, steadying himself, waiting for the pain to ease, but it never did completely.

Realizing that he would have to make do with just three legs, he slowly stepped forward, putting one of his front legs before the other and pushing off with his one healthy hind leg.

A short walk that usually took three seconds with little trouble now took a few minutes of considerable effort mixed with misery. Finally making it to his water, he drank until the bowl was empty. A bite mark on his tongue kept the strong taste of blood in his mouth, but he was able to kill his thirst.

The injured Lab carefully dragged his broken leg behind him, making his way to the front of the house. Using his two front legs, he pulled himself underneath the porch to his safe place. Hurting and terrified, he needed to hide from the world, not knowing that doing so would prolong his suffering.

10

BROKEN

Tom pulled into his driveway, relieved to be home. It had been a long, grueling day at work. A day where he had earned every cent of his salary. Where plans became issues and issues became problems.

Getting out of his truck, he felt relieved knowing supper was ready in the refrigerator. He and Hope had bought takeout from Fatbacks the night before and only eaten half of what they ordered.

Tom locked the gate door behind him, turned toward the house and noticed that all the food he'd left Rex that morning was still in his feed bowl.

"Well, that's odd," he said aloud. He also noticed Rex's yellow duck resting in the same rocking chair just as it had that morning before he left for work. That was also unusual.

Lucky stayed inside the house that morning because it was pouring rain. Tom recalled that he hadn't seen his Lab before he left for work, but he remembered thinking it was because the young dog was under the house, trying to avoid the weather.

He called out to Rex while he walked toward the front porch steps. scanning the yard for signs of his dog while listening for any sounds from underneath the house. Rex was a heavy sleeper, and sometimes he fell asleep under the house and didn't wake up right away after being called.

Tom continued to the front door and wasn't surprised to hear Lucky on the other side as he put the key into the lock. When he opened the door, he saw an anxious little dog sitting beside his feed bowl, which had been dragged into the middle of the living room.

"Patience is not your strong suit, is it, little man?"

He knew it would be dark soon, so he wasted no time feeding Lucky so he could search for Rex. Hopefully, it wouldn't take long to find him, but the more he thought about it, the more worried he became.

"I guess the leftovers from Fatbacks will have to wait a little while longer," he said to himself.

He quickly changed out of his work clothes into a pair of jeans, an old shirt and boots. While he pulled his boots onto his feet, he thought of how Rex loved swimming in the pond. Maybe he found a way out of the fence and went for a swim, he thought.

"That crazy dog may have spent the afternoon jumping off that old pier," Tom said with a smile.

Shutting the house door behind him, he yelled Rex's name again, hoping for a different result, but he heard the same silence and an old pickup truck driving by.

He walked around the house to see if anything was out of place, but nothing seemed to be. It was clear that the dog wasn't inside the fence, so Tom figured the pond was as good a place as any to start looking. He walked toward the back gate, digging into his pockets for the key.

Once he opened it, he called out to Rex again, this time louder and in the direction of the pond. It wasn't visible from the house, and it was far enough away that Tom wasn't sure Rex would hear him even if he was at the pier.

He could only wonder what might have happened. Every time Tom called out for his dog with no good result, it made him worry more. Rex had never tried to escape the fence before. He wondered if someone had opened the gate and let him out.

"Who would do that?" he thought. It didn't make sense.

Tom felt that the young Lab would have met him at the gate that afternoon if he could have, even if he had found a way out of the fence. That meeting in the yard every afternoon always seemed to be one of the highlights of Rex's day. Could someone have stolen him? That would explain him missing, but who would bother to steal a dog? Nothing was missing or out of place around the house.

Tom yelled Rex's name again, stopping to see or hear anything that might be a clue to his whereabouts.

He finally made it to the pond, but there was no sign of his dog. Half-expecting to see a soaking wet Rex lying on the pier, he called out once more but received no answer.

The pond was about an acre and a half in size, surrounded by tall pine trees and water oaks. Half of the area around it was accessible and easily fishable. The other half was grown with weeds and smaller, unrecognizable trees that would never amount to anything but nuisance and shade.

The surface of the pier was dry, which led Tom to believe that Rex hadn't been there that afternoon. As he stood looking and listening, he saw a big bass strike the top of the water at the opposite end of the fishing hole. The only other noticeable sound was the water running through the spillway on the other side of the dam.

Tom hoped against hope that his dog had found a way out of the fence and was enjoying himself playing around the water. Deciding he had reached a dead end, he turned to head back to the house.

After only a few steps, he thought about the three dead puppies he and Rex had buried several months prior.

"Could that be the answer?" he thought to himself.

He knew the young dog had been affected by seeing those puppies. There had been a few times since then that Tom noticed his young Lab returning to that tree and hanging out. It was almost like he was paying his respects.

Daylight was fading fast. Tom didn't want to be trouncing around in those woods after dark. The area he would be walking through had never been cleared nor cut because it sat in a bottom that stayed wet. Making matters worse, he had left the house in such a hurry that he hadn't thought to grab his shotgun, or as he liked to call it, his "snake repellant."

Tom made long, fast strides toward the tree where those puppies lay buried, only occasionally slowing down to navigate his way through the brush, thorny bushes, and small oaks. If Rex was at that tree, Tom wanted to find him and make it back home before it was completely dark.

He heard the woods around him come alive as the sun slowly disappeared. Locusts, frogs, and crickets were beginning their nightly conversations with one another. He remembered hearing those same sounds growing up around that pond, but even as a kid, he always made sure he was back at Grandma's house before dark.

Tom finally saw the pine tree he was working so hard to reach. He recognized the odd-looking, crooked limb that hung down the otherwise perfect tree.

He slowed his pace, being extra careful where his feet landed. The last thing he needed was to step on a rattlesnake, especially this far from the house.

About twenty yards from the pine, he realized that his idea wasn't going to pan out. There was no dog to be seen or heard. The spot where the puppies lay was precisely as he and Rex had left it several months before. He called out to Rex just for the heck of it but didn't see or hear an answer.

Stumbling through the darkness, Tom realized that he was now in the exact situation he had wanted to avoid. At this point, he could barely see where he was stepping. To make matters worse, a noise that sounded like a panther screaming could be heard in the distance. He recalled his dad telling him stories about seeing huge black cats in those woods when he was a kid. He couldn't imagine something worse than crossing paths with one of those cats right now.

The scarce light available, provided by a quarter moon hovering in the sky, was partially blocked by clouds.

"A flashlight would have been a great idea," he mumbled as he shifted through the growth.

His mission had now changed from finding Rex to making it home without seeing a snake or becoming a black panther's next menu item.

Fighting through the growth and barely able to see past arm's length, he could now see the security lights in his yard through the trees.

"That's what I needed to see," he said aloud. He felt his heartbeat slow as he walked closer to home.

The idea of Rex being on the front porch waiting for him made its way into Tom's mind once he felt confident that he wouldn't be eaten by a panther. Wouldn't it be something if that crazy dog was sitting by the front door holding that duck when I got back, he thought.

"This could be a funny story that I tell everybody at work tomorrow," he said.

He closed and locked the back gate behind him. Still thinking the night could have a happy ending, he walked along the side of the house toward the front yard. He turned the corner and looked toward the front porch, but no happy reunion was waiting for him.

On the porch, he reached for Rex's yellow duck. The idea that he might never see that silly black Lab again flooded his mind. He couldn't help but wonder if he could have done something different. If he had taken the time this morning to look for him before he left for work, would things be different now?

Tom reached down and squeezed the stuffed duck so it would make that annoying squeaking sound that Rex loved so much. After the duck said its piece, he threw it out into the front yard.

Tom heard his phone ringing inside. He quickly made his way into the house. It was Hope.

"Hello," Tom answered.

"Hey, where have you been? I've been calling you all afternoon."

Tom told her about the not-so-enjoyable walk he had just finished.

Hope did her best to cheer him up, and it worked for the most part. She had a way of being encouraging without being obvious about it. Tom felt better after he hung up, but he was still starving and exhausted. He almost forgot about the food from Fatbacks inside the refrigerator. Leftovers never sounded so good, he thought.

The last thing Tom thought about before he went to sleep that night and the first thing he thought about when he woke up the next morning was his missing Lab.

He had decided the night before to set his alarm clock an hour earlier so he would have extra time to ride around and look for his dog. Although he didn't want to consider it, Tom realized that Rex could be lying along the road somewhere. Finding his dog dead was not how Tom wanted to start his day, but he knew it was a possibility.

He hurried through the motions of getting ready for work and satisfying Lucky with a can of cat food for breakfast and fresh water in his bowl. He made himself a peanut butter and jelly sandwich along with a cold glass of milk. The plan was to eat while he drove, giving him extra time to search.

The usual morning routine had Rex sitting on the front porch and waiting for Tom to walk out with breakfast. When the front door opened that morning, there was no dog.

"I wouldn't be that fortunate," Tom said to himself.

As he walked to the porch steps, he looked toward the front yard.

"Where did that stuffed duck go? I know I tossed that duck into the front yard last night just before I went inside," he argued with himself.

Tom stood there several seconds while he scanned the whole yard for the toy. At that moment, he realized that he had failed to look in the most obvious place for his dog—where Rex always went when he saw trouble coming.

He darted around to the front of the house. Getting on all fours at one corner of the front porch, he yelled out Rex's name, hoping he was about to solve the mystery of his missing dog.

As Tom's eyes adjusted from the bright and sunny morning to the black that filled the space beneath his house, he realized the search was over. Even though his eyes were still fighting the darkness, he could see Rex's silhouette in the same corner Tom had pulled him from as a puppy. Rex had gone to his safe place, the place he went whenever problems became too complicated too quickly.

Tom's relief covered him like a soft, warm blanket. He didn't care that Rex had caused a wild goose chase the evening before. All was forgiven the second his eyes saw that Lab sitting in that familiar corner.

Tom couldn't help but smile as his relief turned to joy. Within a matter of minutes, he had traveled through several different emotions, from wondering whether Rex would ever be seen again to knowing that Rex was not only alive, but also safe at home.

"Rex, what are you doing under there, buddy?" Tom asked.

The young Lab made no attempt to move.

"Come here, boy!" Tom begged as he tapped on the ground.

Rex made no movement or sound. The only response Tom could get out of his young Lab was a blank stare.

"What's wrong?" He knew now that something wasn't right.

Rex's solid black coat and the lack of light made it difficult for Tom to get a good look at the young dog.

"Hold on, boy, let me get a flashlight so I can get a better look at you."

He wasted no time getting the light from his truck. Once back, Tom dropped on all fours again and shined the light into the corner.

The first thing the light found was the yellow duck lying in front of Rex. Tom shined the light on Rex's face just for a half-second before noticing red glistening from one of the dog's back legs. He knew he was looking at dried blood—lots of it. It looked like it came from a wound on Rex's hip.

Tom called out to his young Lab once more. This time, Rex seemed to snap out of the shock controlling him. He finally acknowledged his human there.

The injured dog tried to stand, but his body would not allow it. He let out a whimper as he eased back into a sitting position.

"Boy, what happened to your hip?" Tom asked.

Like before, Tom's voice seemed to encourage Rex to stand, this time by using his two front legs he dragged himself forward enough to stand with help from only one hind leg.

Once Rex stood, his right leg dangled loosely from his bloody hip like it was being held to his body by strings.

Tom's relief and joy were quickly becoming shock and concern. He didn't know how Rex had ended up this way, but he knew the faster he could get him to Dr. Wright, the better.

"Come on, Rex, come to me, buddy," Tom encouraged.

Hearing Tom's voice, the injured Lab let out another whimper and slowly picked up his yellow duck out of the dirt, battling soreness and pain he began gingerly limping toward Tom, keeping the back half of his body upright with his one good hind leg and letting the injured leg drag partially on the ground.

Tom quickly decided that the best way to get Rex from under the porch was to allow him to walk out on his own. The porch was so low that there was no way Tom could carry him out, and he didn't want to drag him out either. Watching Rex limp toward him was painful for Tom, but he could only imagine the pain Rex felt with every step.

Every couple of steps, the injured Lab stopped and looked at Tom as if asking for encouragement.

"Come on, boy, just a few more."

As the Lab got closer, Tom saw more of the damage Rex was fighting to overcome. One area on one of his front legs had no fur or skin, just exposed tissue. There was a similar spot on one of his front shoulders. The more Tom saw, the more concerned he became.

Finally, Rex made it to the edge of the porch. Tom backed up and patted the ground to encourage Rex to keep moving toward him. After a couple more steps, Rex dropped his yellow duck on the ground.

Ignoring the blood, Tom steadied himself and slowly lifted Rex, mindful of his broken leg. He could feel his young dog trembling but didn't know if it was from the cold or fear.

"Okay, buddy, let's go get you some help."

Rex made no sound, but once Tom turned to walk, he felt Rex's body completely relax in his arms. As he carried his young Lab, Tom wondered how long he had been under the porch.

"You're safe now," Tom said as he opened the truck door.

In Dr. Wright's waiting room, Tom stood looking out a window at two squirrels searching for acorns under a big oak tree. He thought about how relieved he was that there had been no county deputies or state troopers on his path to the doctor's office. He wasn't sure how many traffic laws he had broken getting to Dr. Wright's, but he knew it was more than a few.

It had been about twenty minutes since the nurse took Rex back to the X-ray room. The office wasn't open yet, but Tom knew that the nurses typically got there early.

Dr. Wright's voice could be heard as he came through the back door only a few minutes after Tom and Rex arrived. The old doc wasn't a soft-spoken person, so it was easy to know when he was in the building.

After a few more minutes, the door to the examination room quickly swung open, allowing Dr. Wright to walk through.

"Good morning, Tom. What in the hell happened to Rex?"

"I wish I knew. I found him like that this morning. Is he going to be okay?"

Dr. Wright pulled a cigar from his lab coat and stuck it in his mouth. "Follow me outside, so I can smoke part of this cancer stick before it gets too crazy around here."

Outside, Dr. Wright lit his cigar and took a quick draw from it. "Okay, your dog is beat to hell and back. If I had to guess, I'd say he was hit by a car. We cleaned gravel out of his wounds, but I also found a bite mark of some kind on one of his legs. Since he's so beaten up, I took several different X-rays to look for any internal damage. Best I can tell, all the major organs are fine. I didn't find anything that concerns me. His heart rate and blood pressure are higher than normal, but I think that's due to the pain from his leg plus the fact that he's scared to death. We cleaned all the wounds, and a couple of places will need stitches. Now, about that leg: it's fractured in three different places. One of those fractures is not a clean break. It's more like that part of the bone has been crushed. I'm not sure what happened exactly, but I know that leg took the worse of it. Tom, you have a decision to make," Dr. Wright said, blowing cigar smoke straight up in the air.

"What do you mean?" asked Tom.

The doctor took another draw from his cigar and dispatched the smoke toward the ground this time. "We can't leave that leg as is. He would never fully regain the use of it, and it would always cause him pain. Down the road, it could cause significant problems, so it wouldn't be fair to Rex to leave it as is."

Tom nodded in agreement.

"You've got three choices," Dr. Wright continued. "You can take him to a surgeon and let them try to repair the leg. Looking at the X-ray, that might work and it might not. There's a guy in Auburn I recommend. But this would be the most expensive option. The second option is to amputate the leg. I can do that for you here in my office. As long as everything goes well, he would be back home in three or four days. He would need to be watched closely for a few days and kept inside, but after a few weeks, he should be back doing normal dog things," Dr. Wright explained.

"So what's the third option?"

"The third option is to put him down," Dr. Wright answered.

"But he's so young."

"Well, that's my least favorite choice of the three, but it is an option."

"How much would it cost to have his leg amputated?" Tom asked.

"With what we have already done today, you're looking at around six hundred dollars. Of course, we can work out a payment plan that fits your budget."

Tom didn't have an extra six hundred dollars lying around, but he knew a surgeon would cost a lot more. He also knew he didn't like the idea of having Rex put down.

"Look, if you need time to think about it, you can call me later today. We've given Rex something for the pain, so he's comfortable for now. I've got to get in here and get my day started," the doctor explained.

Tom thought about it for half a second. "Go ahead and take it off; I'll find the money from somewhere."

Dr. Wright put out his cigar with the bottom of his shoe.

"Man, I'm glad you said that. The last thing I need at my house is another three-legged animal."

Tom walked out of the clinic relieved that Rex would be okay. Maybe he hadn't realized it before, but the last twelve hours proved that he had formed a bond with his young Lab. A bond that just cost him six hundred dollars.

11

A TRUE FRIEND

The sound of rain hitting the tin roof echoed throughout the house as Tom sat in his recliner reading the newspaper from the day before. Lucky was still fast asleep in the middle of the bed under the covers, not concerned about the rain or the occasional thunder that could be heard in the distance.

Tom had woken up two hours earlier from a deep sleep but couldn't make himself fall back there no matter how hard he tried.

Today was Friday, and a busy day awaited him but not for the usual reasons. He was using a vacation day from work to prepare for a fishing trip he helped organize three months prior.

The plan was for him and Mike to drive down to the Gulf later that day and meet some old friends from high school for a weekend of seafood and deep-sea fishing. When he first made these plans, Tom had no way of knowing that he would have a dog lying in his living room who was only days removed from an amputation.

Fortunately, Hope agreed to watch Lucky that weekend and had no problem taking care of Rex as well.

"Those two dogs will be fine. Go and have a good time," Hope promised.

Tom continued to sit and enjoy the sounds that the wind and rain made with his old house, but he knew he needed to get up and start his day. Daylight was slower than usual to happen because of the rain and clouds, but it was gradually on its way.

Rex was lying on a makeshift bed Tom made by cutting an old memory foam mattress into quarters. It was the seventh day since the surgery and his second day at home. Dr. Wright had assured Tom that with time, Rex would eventually not even realize that he was missing a leg.

Tom wasn't sure if Dr. Wright's prediction would come true. However, he was certain that the dog he knew before the surgery was not the dog lying on his living room floor that morning. Even Dr. Wright had noticed a difference in Rex and kept him an extra day but found nothing to blame for his lack of energy. The old doctor felt that beyond the cuts and obvious sore places, nothing was physically wrong with the Lab.

"Rex's spirit is missing," Tom had told Hope the night before.

The dog that wouldn't be still, the dog that steadily ran and played was now content to lie on his mattress and stare at the floor. Even Lucky tried to get a reaction from the young Lab by grabbing his yellow duck and wrestling with it the previous night, but Rex seemed uninterested.

As Tom walked through the dining room, he heard Rex let out a whimper mixed with a groan.

"You okay, boy?" Tom asked from the kitchen. "I guess it's time for one of your pain pills."

The surgery wasn't the only reason for the pills. The young Lab's body was full of cuts and sore spots. Exposed areas of skin were visible, some made even more noticeable by stitches. There were wounds on his legs and hips that would become lifelong scars.

Tom pushed the pain pill into a hot dog wiener and dropped it at Rex's feet. "Maybe when some of this pain is gone, you will feel more like your old self," he said, scratching his young dog under his chin.

Rex gave Tom what looked like an appreciative gaze, then laid his head back down on the mattress.

Before he made it back to the kitchen, Lucky hit the floor. The sound of little toenails hitting the linoleum bounced throughout the house.

"Well, you finally decided to grace us with your presence," Tom joked.

His words did nothing to faze the old dog as he headed toward his feed bowl for a taste of water. Tom knew what was coming next, so he reached for a can of cat food, opened it, and dumped it in the spoiled dog's bowl.

According to the forecast, the rain and thunder would move out that morning, allowing the skies to clear up ahead of a beautiful weekend. The more Tom thought about it, the more he looked forward to getting away from home and work for a couple of days.

He spent the morning packing food, clothes, and fishing gear.

Lucky wasn't happy. The old dog had been around long enough to know when Tom was preparing to go somewhere. Even though the little guy acted like he didn't care much for Tom at times, he didn't enjoy the idea of being left behind.

The morning passed with the rain stopping and the clouds moving out of the sun's way. It seemed the forecast Tom saw was coming true.

Other than going outside for a bathroom break, Rex stayed on his mattress and slept. The young dog didn't act very interested in anything happening inside the house that morning.

Tom loaded the last cooler on his truck and shut the tailgate. The only thing left to do was load Rex and Lucky up so he could drop them off at Hope's on his way to pick up Mike.

A few minutes later, he walked back into the house, grabbed Rex's leash, and hooked it to the young Lab's collar.

"Okay, boy, let's get you to the truck."

Once Rex was off his mattress, Tom pulled him toward the front door. In the five days since Rex's surgery, he had learned how to walk using only three legs, but at times it was still tricky, and he wasn't the fastest three-legged dog ever, at least not yet.

Tom patiently led the young Lab to the truck, stopping once for Rex to do his business and once more just because Rex decided to sit down. The endless energy Rex once carried around with him seemed to be gone. The playful attitude he had displayed time after time was no longer there. As Tom walked with Rex to the truck, he thought about when he had scolded Rex for being too playful; he now found himself missing those moments.

When they reached the truck, Tom carefully lifted Rex and slowly placed him in the backseat. "I hope riding back here doesn't make you carsick."

Hope was no stranger to babysitting. She had grown up watching two younger sisters, but she was a little nervous about taking care of someone else's dogs, especially one that had just undergone surgery. She never told Tom about her concerns; she knew he needed a break and would do what she could to make sure he got it.

She sat patiently in a rocking chair on her front porch, waiting for the new guest. Her home was an old, white, two-story antebellum house that she was slowly bringing back to life with a renovation. Hope had bought the old house at an estate sale almost by accident. She had gone to the auction that day looking for antiques, but only three people placed bids on the house, and to her surprise, her offer was the highest. Tom jokingly told her that the old house was the biggest antique available that day.

The downstairs part of the house was almost finished, but the upstairs still needed a lot of work. Hope lived in the downstairs area and used the upstairs for storage. She sometimes joked that she'd bought two houses that day that just happened to be stacked on top of one another.

Tom pulled into the driveway and saw Hope sitting on the porch in an old, red, flannel shirt and faded blue jeans.

"Maybe I should just stay here this weekend," he said to himself.

Tom had always thought Hope was a special kind of pretty, and she did nothing that morning to change his mind.

Hope walked to the truck to help him bring in what he had packed for the two pups.

"My gosh, this is a lot to unload! How long are you going to be gone?" Hope asked with a smile.

"Well, you never know, I could have so much fun down there that I may decide to stay a few extra days," Tom answered with a sly grin.

"I know better than that. I'm doing good to get rid of you for the weekend," Hope fired back.

Hope grabbed Lucky, and Tom grabbed an oversized garbage bag full of dog stuff. They headed inside the house.

"Where's Rex?" Hope asked.

"He's in the backseat."

"I didn't even see or hear him. How is he?"

"He's the same; all he wants to do is lie on his bed and sleep. He has an appetite, he drinks enough water, but he has no desire to do anything beyond that. His pain medicine is here in the bag. He gets three a day. I give him his third one just before bedtime, so he doesn't wake up during the night hurting. He has a lot of sore spots other than where those stitches are, so I've been letting him move at his pace. He's good about sounding the alarm when he needs to go outside. If you let him out just before bedtime, he should be good until morning."

When Tom made it back to the truck, Rex was whimpering but still lying in the same spot he had begun the ride in.

"Boy, did you think I forgot about you?" Tom asked as he slowly slid his arm under the young Lab and lifted him off the seat.

Rex gradually made it to the house minus his one leg. Inside, he looked around as if he was soaking in his new environment.

"Okay, boy, this is going to be home for the next couple days," Tom said, unhooking the dog from his leash.

Hope encouraged Tom not to worry. She promised she would call him if she had a major problem. As she watched Tom back down her driveway, she felt satisfied that he was going on his trip but still uneasy about the upcoming weekend.

Hope had spent the previous week getting ready to dog sit. The house was clean, groceries bought, and the grass cut. She planned it so she wouldn't even have to leave the house unless something unexpected happened.

There was an upside to having all the weekend chores done before the weekend. She planned to read a book she had bought a month ago but hadn't started. She had also bought a couple of movies a few weeks ago that she planned on watching, plus there was a closet that she felt needed a makeover.

The afternoon went by quickly and quietly. Lucky and Rex both slept most of it away.

Hope started reading her book and stole a quick nap on the sofa. Tom mentioned to her several times that Lucky would have no problem reminding her about supper time if she forgot. He told her that by six o'clock Lucky would find his bowl and set off his food alarm. He wasn't wrong about Lucky's food alarm, but it sounded off an hour early.

Hope walked into the kitchen, and there the old dog stood before his empty bowl, barking up a storm.

"Is your stomach growling, little man?"

Rex rested on his mattress in the living room in front of the fireplace. He hadn't moved much or made a sound since Tom left. Hope walked out of the kitchen and accidentally made eye contact with the black Lab. She couldn't help but feel sorry for him, but at the same time, she thought of what a pretty animal he was.

She walked over to where he lay and sat beside him, her legs stretched out in front of her, and started lightly scratching his back. Rex slowly lifted his head and rested it on her left leg.

"Being sweet will get you everywhere, young man," Hope said as she continued to scratch. Sitting there, she realized she almost forgotten that he had been born without a tail.

"Boy, I haven't seen you wag that nub in a long time. We are going to have to do something about that this weekend."

The next morning, the house was quiet as sunlight began to filter through the blinds. Rex was awake but waiting patiently for Hope to appear so he could go outside and take care of his business. Hope, still in bed but awake, enjoyed the sounds of an almost empty house.

She had decided before she went to bed the night before that if Lucky wanted to sleep with her, she wouldn't fight him. The old dog was under the covers, almost dead center of the bed. Hope quickly realized that sleeping with Lucky was like sleeping with a heating pad, but she managed a good night's sleep regardless.

It occurred to her that she hadn't heard a sound from Rex all night.

"I guess I better check on the patient. Whatcha think, Lucky?"

After getting no response from her bedfellow, she let herself have one more big stretch and gently eased out of bed, trying not to disturb the old dog.

In her purple pajamas and fuzzy white slippers, she headed to the living room, performing a new stretch every few steps.

Rex heard her coming and let out a bark.

"There he is," Hope yelled as she grabbed his leash off the coffee table.

Rex pushed himself up into a sitting position and waited.

"Good morning, sweet boy!" Hope attached the leash to the young dog and gave a gentle pull toward the front door.

As Rex stood, Hope noticed his little nub beginning to twitch back and forth. A huge smile bloomed on Hope's face.

"Are you wagging that nub at me?" she asked as she kneeled before Rex and rubbed his neck and head. "That's just what I wanted to see this morning."

The injured Lab was slow and deliberate with his movements on his way to the front door, sometimes looking at Hope as if he needed ideas about which direction to move in.

"Okay, boy, no excuses. You have the whole yard to pick and choose from."

The yard was full of flowers, trees, bushes, and freshly cut grass. It was a buffet of scents coming from every direction. Before the surgery,

Rex would have checked out every bush, smelled every flower, and rubbed against every tree. He would have exhausted himself investigating every inch of his temporary home. Instead, he walked to the nearest bush, did his business, and started walking back toward the front door of the house.

"Rex, are you sure that's all you need to do?" Hope asked.

Rex gave no response as he kept walking to the house.

"Not so fast, Mister," Hope said as she slightly pulled back on the leash. "Let's stay out here and enjoy the fresh air for a few minutes. I know you've been cooped up inside for the better part of a week. Being outside might make you feel better."

Hope had good reason to want to enjoy the outside. With the temperature around sixty-five degrees, it was a beautiful, sunny morning with a light breeze from the north that kept the humidity away. It was the opposite of the rain and thunder from the previous morning.

Rex, on the other hand, didn't seem as enthused about being away from his bed, but he did check out a few more flowers, and Hope managed to get another nub-wagging out of him.

"Slowly but surely, my sweet boy, I'm going to put you in a better mood," she told the injured Lab. She then led him back inside the house.

As she returned Rex's leash to the coffee table, Hope heard a bark from the kitchen.

"So his majesty has decided to get up!" Hope yelled.

She walked into the kitchen and found Lucky sitting at his feed bowl, staring back at her.

"You know, you could learn some manners from Rex," Hope said. She cracked open the can of cat food from the cabinet.

"Okay, Rex needs some breakfast too," she said, pulling a bowl from the refrigerator. The day before, she had baked a few sweet potatoes so Rex could have them during the weekend. She placed two of them on a plate, placing it in the microwave. The aroma of the cinnamon and potatoes covered the downstairs part of the house.

Once the scent reached Rex, he let out a bark. By the time the buzzer on the microwave sounded, the hungry Lab was standing in the kitchen waiting for his breakfast.

"Well, I see that food still motivates you," Hope said. She opened the microwave door and pulled out the plate to set it on the kitchen counter. She then opened a can of dog food and emptied half of it onto the plate beside the sweet potatoes.

"Okay, eat up," she said.

Hope spent the rest of the morning giving that closet the make-over she had planned. She cleaned both bathrooms and emptied all the garbage cans throughout the house.

Lucky and Rex slept their morning away. After she finished her garbage duty, Hope walked into the living room to check on her guest.

"You two are being mighty quiet in here," she said.

Rex raised his head from the floor. Lucky didn't move a muscle. Hope stood still for a second, then said "cat food" loud enough for Lucky to hear. The curious old dog quickly jumped up as if something had tried to grab him.

As midday became afternoon, Hope took a power nap on the couch with Lucky asleep at her feet. She awoke to hear thunder from a storm that seemed to come out of nowhere but was strong enough to cause the lights to blink on and off.

Glad that the two dogs were there to keep her mind off the storm, she got up from the couch and walked into the kitchen looking for something to snack on. She stopped at the kitchen window and looked outside.

"Yep, it's definitely about to storm out there," she told herself. She spent the next few minutes placing a candle in each of the downstairs rooms in case the house lost power.

Two hours later, the storm was an afterthought as Hope led Rex back into the house from a trip outside. Both Lucky and Rex were fed and finishing their last bathroom break of the day. Hope was tired;

aside from her nap just before the storm came, she had been on her feet moving around for the whole day.

"Okay, guys, I don't care if it is still light outside. I'm about to take me a shower and go to bed. It's been a long day," she said as she turned off the porch light.

Hope figured there was no reason for Rex to sleep in the living room by himself, so she pulled his mattress into her bedroom. She again decided it would be easier to start the night letting Lucky sleep with her.

Hope walked out of the kitchen and into the bedroom with Rex's medicine pushed inside a piece of sweet potato.

"Here ya go, boy," she said as she dropped it by his bed. Rex swallowed the treat, never knowing there was anything inside.

With Lucky already snoring in the middle of her bed and Rex lying quietly beside the bedroom door, Hope reached and turned out the lamp on her nightstand. She was ready for sleep; the first day of dog sitting had been a success. What she didn't know was that the next day would not be so easy.

The second half of the weekend started out like the first. Hope got up and made sure both dogs were fed and watered. She gave Rex his medicine and drank her first cup of coffee. While working on her second cup of joe, she realized that she hadn't checked on her vegetable garden the day before.

"I bet I have tomatoes and okra that need to be gathered. I forgot about that garden yesterday," she said to herself just before she enjoyed the last swallow of coffee from her cup.

The only thing Hope enjoyed more than working in her yard was working in her garden. The garden was close to nine hundred square feet in size, and she invested a lot of time planting and taking care of her vegetable plants. It included several different types of peppers, okra, and tomatoes. She also had squash and eggplant.

She decided it might do Rex and Lucky good to get out and enjoy the outside some that morning. Both dogs had spent most of the day inside the house the day before.

Wearing an old, pink T-shirt and an old pair of faded cargo pants, she grabbed an oversized sun hat to protect her face and ears from the sun. The thought of seeing what was waiting in the garden made her happy. She loved the idea that every time she walked down there, she saw something different, ready to be cooked and eaten.

Hope led both dogs across the back porch and down the back steps. She then grabbed two empty five-gallon buckets that sat at the bottom of the steps.

"Come on, guys, let's go," Hope encouraged.

As soon as Lucky's feet hit the grass, he jogged over to a rosebush, lifted a hind leg, and started wetting the ground beneath it.

Rex stood at the bottom of the back-porch steps and looked around as if he was soaking everything in. The young Lab acted like he didn't trust himself to walk on his three remaining legs.

Finished at the rosebush, Lucky jogged toward the rows of vegetables. Hope turned and saw that Rex was still standing by himself, not moving.

"Rex, come on, boy," she called to him.

Hearing her call, the young, three-legged dog began to walk toward Hope. These were the first steps he had made without someone leading him with a leash since the amputation. He took a few steps and stopped. He took a few more and stopped again. He then took another step and began to jog a bit toward Hope. His remaining back leg supported half his weight as he trotted toward the garden.

"That's it, Rex, keep coming."

Hope was right about her vegetables being ready. The okra needed cutting, the squash required picking, and the tomatoes needed pulling.

"I may not have enough buckets," Hope said to herself.

This was Rex's first experience in a vegetable garden. As he sat there, he picked up scents he had never smelled before and saw unfamiliar plants and blooms. Fat, red tomatoes hung from tall green vines tied to wooden stakes driven into the ground. Long, curly pods protruded away from the tall okra plants. Yellow squash lay hidden under the green leaves of the squash plants.

Lucky seemed to enjoy sticking his nose under each squash plant to see what lay beneath.

"Too bad you can't pick those squash you're finding," Hope said as she pulled tomatoes and tossed them into her bucket.

Rex began to do some exploring of his own, walking through the tomato rows and licking and smelling the ones he could reach. When he came to the okra rows, he bit a large pod of okra in half and quickly dropped it on the ground.

It didn't take Hope long to realize that she needed more buckets. She grabbed the two that were full and started walking toward the house. She lost a few squash on the way, but she didn't bother to stop and save them.

While Hope walked back to the house, Rex and Lucky stayed behind and continued to smell and look around. The old house dog finished his investigation of the squash and started a new one in the rows of tomatoes. Rex sat between two rows of okra and watched Lucky sniff the bottom of each plant and stop at every third one or so to scratch the dirt around it.

It didn't take Hope long to be on her way back with two empty buckets. She could see Rex watching over Lucky, and she could barely see the lap dog's head and tail above the squash plants that stood between them.

As she walked closer, she heard Lucky began to bark. It was a different bark than the one he used inside the house when he was hungry. Louder and more intense, these barks had a different purpose. Hope knew that Lucky must have found something that bothered him but had no idea what it was. It could have been anything from a harmless small frog to a not-so-harmless raccoon.

Rex rose to his feet, the fur between his shoulder blades standing straight up as he started to walk toward Lucky. After a few more steps, Hope saw, Rex's walk became a jog, and she knew that Rex did not like what he saw.

She called out to Lucky, but that didn't stop the old dog from fussing at whatever he saw. The small, black dog didn't back down from much, so Hope didn't expect him to calm down until he was good and ready.

Not knowing what the two dogs were reacting to, she then called out to Rex, but it fell on deaf ears as the three-legged Lab's jog toward his old friend sped up. She dropped the two empty buckets on the ground and began to run toward the garden, knowing Rex would reach Lucky before she would.

Hope would later say that the next ten seconds seemed to happen in slow motion. She made it to the edge of the garden and saw what was causing all the ruckus. Lucky was having a staring contest with a brown and black snake that was coiled up, waiting for a good reason to strike. With only about three feet separating the aggravated snake and the overconfident lapdog, what Hope saw next made her stop running and stand where she was in disbelief.

Understanding the danger Lucky was in, Rex gained more speed the closer he came to the old dog and the coiled snake. For a moment it seemed the young, three-legged Lab had forgotten about his missing leg. From where Hope stood, it looked as if Lucky, so preoccupied with the snake, didn't care that a full-grown Lab was galloping toward him at full speed.

After working as hard as he had ever worked to run with his eyes zoomed in on the snake, Rex locked his two front legs in place, digging his feet into the dirt and causing himself to slide between Lucky and the angry reptile. Knocking his old friend out of harm's way, he somehow grabbed the snake's body with his mouth. He shook the snake violently as he came to a complete stop and ended the crazy encounter by slinging the unwanted visitor away from Lucky into the squash rows.

Landing awkwardly on the ground the snake wanted no more of the black Lab and quickly slithered in the opposite direction out of the garden. Lucky sat there and continued to bark at Rex as if he was telling him that he didn't need his help.

Hope, shocked at what she had just seen, ran toward the two dogs. "Rex, you okay, boy?"

Rex stood there, looking in the direction of the weeds that the snake had escaped through. He turned toward Hope with his bright pink tongue hanging out of the side of his mouth and dirt embedded on the side of his face. As blood dripped down his snout, he started walking toward her but tripped over one of his front legs and stumbled to the ground. Hope saw the blood and knew what had just happened. The snake had managed to strike Rex during the scuffle.

Now Hope's adrenaline started to flow. Not considering the dog's weight, she picked up the Lab and started running toward the car with him. She hadn't seen enough of the snake to know whether it was poisonous, but she was not going to take any chances.

"Come on, Lucky," she yelled as she ran along the side of the house toward the front yard, carrying Rex. Knowing something wasn't right, Lucky scooted behind her and flew up the front porch steps to be let into the safety of the house.

Hope set Rex into the backseat of her car, then ran up the porch steps to open the door for Lucky. As she walked back toward the car, she called Dr. Wright from her cell phone.

"Hello," he answered.

"Dr. Wright, this is Hope. I hate to bother you on a Sunday morning, but I'm heading toward your office with a dog that has a snake bite. I saw the snake, but I don't know if it was poisonous. All I know is it was black and brown and looked to be about four foot long."

"How long has it been since the bite happened?" Dr. Wright asked.

"I think about two minutes," Hope guessed as she backed down her driveway.

Dr. Wright asked her several more questions about the dog she was bringing and the snake that bit him. Hope knew only some of the answers. He told Hope he could be at his office in ten minutes. He also encouraged her to drive safely but explained that if the snake was poisonous, then the sooner the dog received the antivenom, the better.

As Hope drove toward the clinic, she wrestled with the idea of calling Tom to let him know what was happening. She thought it might be better to talk to him after Dr. Wright saw Rex so she would have more information.

No sooner had she decided to wait than her phone started to ring. It was Tom. Hope answered, and before Tom could say anything, she began to tell him the whole story about how Rex had saved an ungrateful Lucky from the snake but been bitten in the process.

"So you don't know if the snake was poisonous?" Tom asked.

"I'm praying that it wasn't," she answered. "When are you going to be home?"

"That's why I'm calling. I'm only about fifteen minutes away from your house. The rest of the guys wanted to stay and fish today, but I got sunburned yesterday, so I didn't want to go back out. Mike is catching a ride back with one of the other guys later today."

"I'm so sorry that Rex got in this mess," Hope said, tearing up.

"Hey, this isn't your fault. If anything, it's Lucky's fault for picking a fight with a four-foot-long snake," Tom answered, trying to make her feel better. They decided Tom would meet her at Dr. Wright's office.

Hope sped up the driveway to the clinic. She could see Dr. Wright's old pickup in its usual parking space. Seeing that old truck made her feel like help was a short distance away.

She opened the back door of the car, and before she knew it, Rex jumped out and jogged up to the clinic's front door. Hope noticed that the bite mark on his nose didn't look any worse than it had in the garden. She also saw that the bleeding had stopped.

"That's got to be a good sign," she said as she opened the clinic door.

Dr. Wright was sitting in one of the lobby chairs, holding a syringe full of antivenom.

"That's Rex! This poor dog can't catch a break," he said as he stood from the chair. The old doctor kneeled to one knee in front of

Rex and held his head still so he could get a good look at his snout. "Well, I won't be needing this antivenom," he said with a big smile.

"Are you sure?" Hope asked, taking a deep breath.

"Looks more like a scrape than a bite. I don't see any puncture wounds. There's hardly any swelling. Let's take him into one of the exam rooms. I'll clean the dirt out of the area and give him a shot to help keep down any infection; I already have him on oral antibiotics, so he should be fine. It was probably a chicken snake, but it just grazed him. I'll also check and clean the areas where his stitches are."

Hope sat down in a chair in the corner of the exam room and took a deep breath. As Dr. Wright pulled out a pack of gauze from the cabinet, he heard the front door open and shut.

"Anybody home?" Tom yelled.

Dr. Wright walked back into the lobby.

"Tom, do you realize that Rex has been here so often here lately that if he were a child and this were a hospital emergency room, I'd have to call child services today," Dr. Wright joked.

"How is he?" Tom asked, ignoring the punchline.

"He's going to be okay; the snake wasn't poisonous. What happened to you? You're as red as a lobster."

"Oh, I went fishing yesterday," Tom answered.

"Fishing? Where at, the sun?" The old doctor stepped closer for a better look. "Tom, I don't know if you realize it yet, but you may be in worse shape than the dog. Is the sunburn underneath your shirt also?"

"Yep," Tom slowly answered.

"Go into the room that Rex is in and take off your shirt. We need to see how hot that burn is," Dr. Wright instructed.

As Tom took off his shirt, Dr. Wright started cleaning Rex's wound.

"Hey, you're not going to start with me?" Tom asked.

"Nope, Rex was here first. Besides, from what Hope told me, Rex is a hero. He jumped in between Lucky and that snake. You, on the other hand, just forgot to put on sunscreen," Dr. Wright answered.

Tom shook his head and climbed onto the exam table. As Tom sat there, he noticed a poster on the wall advertising the Jumpathon. "Well, I guess Rex missed his chance to compete in that jump competition," he said.

Dr. Wright looked up from cleaning Rex's snout. "I don't know, Tom. No rule says a dog has to have four legs to compete. As long as you can show that Rex can swim, you can enter him."

"That's a good question. Can a three-legged dog swim?" Tom asked.

"They can, but some prefer not to. I've seen dogs lose a leg and go back in the water as if nothing happened. If the dog loved the water with four legs, then most likely he will love the water with three legs."

Tom thought a minute. "The way Rex has been acting the past few days, I doubt he would do well in any competition."

Hope punched Tom on the arm. "Tom, do you realize that Rex just saved Lucky from a snake? You may be surprised by what he can do."

Dr. Wright kept working with Rex, being as gentle as you could ask him to be.

"Okay, boy, this is going to burn a little bit," he warned. "Hope, do you know the story behind why each dog has to prove they can swim before entering the Jumpathon?"

Hope thought for a second. "It seems like I heard something, but go ahead and tell us."

Dr. Wright began the story of a man from a neighboring town who entered his blue tick hound in the contest.

"It was a beautiful animal," he recalled. "This would have been about five years ago. The dog's owner boasted about how his dog won ribbons in several dog shows across the state. He also bragged about how fast the dog could run and how high he could jump.

"You could tell the gentleman enjoyed bragging about his hound. And of course, he was right: that dog looked like a streak of lighting as he ran toward the edge of the ramp for his first jump. And to be honest, I've never seen a dog leap as high as he did off the ramp that day. It was like he got shot out of a damn cannon," Dr. Wright explained.

"The problem was nobody ever bothered to see if the poor dog could swim. As contest judges, we asked each owner whether their dog could swim, but we didn't make them prove it. The owner just assumed since the dog was so athletic, he would naturally be fine. He never bothered to make sure. I'll never forget what happened when that dog hit the water."

"Well, what happened?" Hope asked.

"He sank to the bottom of the pond. It was like somebody dropped a bowling ball out of an airplane. The poor hound didn't even try to swim. Once he made contact with the water, he didn't have a clue what to do next. He froze stiff as a board. It looked like the dog wanted to drown."

"So what did his owner do?" Tom asked.

"Nothing!" Dr. Wright yelled. "We later found out the owner couldn't swim either."

"Don't tell me the dog drowned," Hope interrupted.

"Ms. Hope, do you think I would have sat there and let that dog drown? Once we saw that the hound wasn't going to save himself, I dove in, picked him up off the pond floor and pulled him to the edge of the water."

"Was he okay?" Tom asked.

"The hapless fellow was terrified but okay. At least he knew enough to hold his breath while he sank to the bottom. At any rate, I'm too old and slow to be jumping in ponds and pulling grown dogs from their death. That's why you have to prove your dog can swim," Dr. Wright said, laughing aloud.

The old doctor finished with Rex and turned his attention to Tom. "Young man, what have you been doing this weekend? You look like death on a soda cracker!"

Tom, caught off guard by Dr. Wright's honesty, tried to explain.

"I didn't get any sleep last night because of this burn. Plus, the bed I was in wasn't very comfortable."

"Okay, let's see what we can see," Dr. Wright said as he looked over Tom's back and shoulders. "Yep, you have a mean sunburn. It's not as bad as I thought it might be, but you still have some second-degree burns here. I'm going to give you some cream that works amazingly on sunburns. It comes from a plant that only grows in southeast Asia, and it will take most of the heat out of your skin."

Hope held her end of the leash as she followed Rex out the front door.

Tom followed Hope. "Doc, I appreciate you helping us this morning."

"Don't thank me until you see my bill," the old doctor said as he closed the door behind them.

Later that afternoon, when it was just Tom and the two dogs in his quiet house, Tom leaned back in his recliner and fell sound asleep dreaming about the fish he had caught the day before.

An hour or so into his nap, Tom was awakened by something nudging at his knee. He rearranged himself in the chair and dozed back off to sleep. But the nudging didn't stop, so he opened his eyes again, this time lifting his head and shoulders to see what was interrupting his nod.

The thought of being irritated quickly vanished when he saw Rex standing beside the chair, ears perked, holding his old, dingy duck in his mouth and poking Tom's leg with his nose.

Tom used the arm of the recliner to let his feet down to the floor, then sat up straight. "Come here, boy," he said, grabbing the young Lab's collar and gently pulling it toward him. Tom started to rub around Rex's neck and head.

"First of all, we need to wash this duck," he said, slightly tugging at the toy while Rex held it in his mouth.

Still holding his toy, Rex sat down in front Tom, tilting his head as if trying to understand the words.

"Second of all, as soon as Dr. Wright okays those wounds to get wet, I think we need to find out how you feel about getting back in the water."

Rex rested his head in Tom's lap, his mouth still gripping the duck.

"This is the Rex I was hoping to see again," Tom said.

12

MOTIVATION

Rex quickly moved from side to side across the bed of Tom's truck, occasionally throwing his head back to let out a loud bark. The black Lab had a good idea where Tom was taking him, and he showed his approval. It had been almost five days since the snake bite incident, and Rex showed no lasting effects other than a small scar on his snout.

Tom was in the driver's seat, glad to hear his dog's excitement over the noise of the truck. Less than two weeks ago, Tom hadn't known if he would ever hear that bark again, so he sat and soaked it in as he drove.

The morning sun had just started making its appearance over the trees as Tom pulled into Fatbacks. On his fishing trip the weekend before, he'd realized there were still two vacation days he needed to take before the end of the month or he'd lose them, so he decided to take that Friday off. Tom figured that morning would be a great time to see how Rex felt about swimming again.

He walked in the front door of Fatbacks and saw the usual suspects perched at the front counter, catching up on and, in some cases, creating gossip.

After hearing the bell ring on the door, each person at the counter turned to see who had just walked in.

"Boy, I wish the food here wasn't so damn good," Tom whispered to himself as the door closed behind him.

He stepped toward the cash register, where Ms. Pearl stood swapping food for money. Ms. Pearl was the head cook, head waitress, and head cashier at Fatbacks. She was also the owner.

"Hello, Tom," she yelled before he recognized her.

"Hello, Ms. Pearl, you doing okay today?"

"I may as well be. Nobody wants to hear me complain," she answered, slipping a roll of money in her apron pocket.

Tom shook his head and smiled. "I called an order in; it should be ready."

Tom took a seat on one of the old front counter stools while he waited for Ms. Pearl to check on his order. Reading a menu to pass the time, he heard the bell ring on the front door. Almost immediately, there was laughter, giggling, and then a familiar voice.

"Oh no," he said to himself.

The voice belonged to Ms. Cash, a widow who was a mainstay at Fatbacks. She also happened to be the biggest holder and spreader of gossip in Oakville. If it occurred in the small town, Ms. Cash knew about it. If she didn't know about it, it wasn't from a lack of trying.

It was odd to go to Fatbacks and not see Ms. Cash at the front counter, spreading her information. Tom had thought he would dodge Ms. Cash that morning; he was wrong.

The only seat available at the front counter was the seat beside him. He began to stand slowly, but it was too late.

"Tom, why are you not at work yet?" Ms. Cash asked as she threw her oversized pink purse on the counter and slid onto the stool.

"They fired me," Tom replied with a serious look.

"They what?" Ms. Cash grabbed Tom by the arm.

"No, I'm just kidding. I have a few vacations days to burn, so I took today off."

"Oh, I see," Ms. Cash answered, looking disappointed.

"I heard some interesting news this morning, Tom, and you are just the person to ask about it," the nosy lady said. She pulled her wallet from her purse and placed it on the counter.

Tom considered forgetting about breakfast and making a run for the front door, but he was somewhat curious about the question she was about to ask of him. "Really? I can't imagine what you could have heard." He knew that, like it or not, he was about to find out.

Besides being the town gossip, Ms. Cash also made it a point to be involved in every local function in Oakville. The Christmas parade, the Halloween carnival, the town Easter egg hunt—you name it, and she sat on the committee that planned it.

The Jumpathon was no different. It was her turn to head the committee that organized and funded the contest, and she was determined that it would be the best one ever.

Before she started her interrogation, Ms. Cash took a sip of the free ice water in front of her. "I heard you might enter your little dog into the Jumpathon this year. I also heard that your dog only has three legs?"

Tom heard some hostility in her voice, which caught him off guard. "I guess me, and Rex are guilty on both charges," he answered with a grin.

"Who is Rex?" Ms. Cash asked.

"Rex is the three-legged black Lab that you seem to be so interested in," Tom answered.

Ms. Pearl pushed her way through the kitchen doors and set Tom's order on the counter. "Sorry for the wait; we are shorthanded this morning, so everything is moving slower than normal."

"No problem, Ms. Pearl, your food is worth waiting for. How much do I owe you?"

Ms. Cash sat and watched Tom slide his wallet into his back pocket and pick up his food.

"Tom, before you go, I need to ask you a question."

"Okay, fire away," Tom replied.

"You are not seriously considering entering that dog in the Jumpathon, are you? I mean, think about it: he's missing a leg, how far could he jump anyway? You do realize that there will be several newspapers from around the state covering the event? I don't want to see you embarrass yourself, but I definitely don't want to see our town be embarrassed."

Tom's face began to redden and feel warm for several reasons, none of which had anything to do with the sunburn that had bothered him the last few days.

Tom placed his food back on the counter and gave Ms. Cash all his attention. He couldn't say what he wanted to say, but he still intended to drive his point across while being as polite as possible.

"Ms. Cash, I appreciate your concern, but I'm convinced that if I enter Rex into this Jumpathon, not only would he not embarrass me or the town, I believe that he would do a fine job representing Oakville no matter who's there to watch. I'm also positive that whatever I decide to do with my dog is none of your business. Now, I've been told that no rule exists that would keep a three-legged dog from competing. Is this right?" Tom asked.

"That's correct, but we've never had this problem before," Ms. Cash answered in a low voice.

Although Tom never raised his voice, the people sitting in Fatbacks heard enough of the conversation to know what it was concerning. He knew that once they left, their discussion would be the talk of the town.

"Ms. Cash, I have some gossip of my own to tell you."

A curious look immediately formed on the old lady's face.

"Okay, what is it?"

Tom gently leaned in closer to Ms. Cash so he could whisper low enough that no one else could hear it. "My three-legged dog, he's also missing his tail." He pulled back from the old lady and smiled. "You have a nice day." He then grabbed the food off the front counter and left.

Tom opened the driver-side door and glanced over into the bed of the truck. Rex was sitting in the middle of the bed, ears perked, staring a hole into the bag of food.

"I guess you're ready for some breakfast?" he asked, still irritated by the conversation that had just ended.

Tom reached into the bag, pulling out a chicken biscuit. Rex let out a bark that everyone inside Fatbacks should have been able to hear.

Tom smiled, "Okay, boy, calm down." He threw the warm biscuit into the bed of the truck and watched as the excited dog made short work of it.

As Rex finished off each crumb that fell his way, Tom noticed Ms. Cash's SUV parked beside his truck. "Well, would you look at that. Somebody has bought four shiny new wheels," he said to himself as he rubbed the top of Rex's head.

Knowing his young Lab carried an affection for sparkling wheels, Tom had an idea. "You know, Rex, you have been on the back of this truck for a while now," he said as he grabbed the dog leash. "I bet you need to go to the little dog's room, don't you?"

Tom hooked the leash to Rex's collar and allowed the young Lab to jump down to the ground. "Okay, boy, go for it," he encouraged as the three-legged Lab sniffed around on the dirt.

Within seconds, Rex made a fast dash to one of the back wheels of Ms. Cash's SUV. He slowly steadied himself and sprayed the bottom half of a back rim while Tom stood there with a satisfying grin.

"I'm beginning to love you, Rex." Tom watched the young dog walk to one of the front wheels for a second spray.

Once Rex had visited all four wheels, Tom loaded him back onto the truck. "You ready to go swimming?" He shut the tailgate.

The young Lab answered by running from side to side, letting out three loud barks.

Driving back, Tom couldn't help but think about the conversation between him and Ms. Cash as he ate his chicken biscuit. "The nerve of that lady," he thought. The more he dwelled on it, the angrier he became.

He also realized that Rex would have the final say about the

Jumpathon. If he was afraid to get back in the water or if he refused to make the jump off the pier, his Jumpathon career would end before it began. That didn't stop Tom from imagining the look on Ms. Cash's face if she saw Rex jump that first day of the contest.

The black Lab knew where they were headed once Tom made the turn down the old logging road that traveled through his land. Rex hadn't been to the pond since his operation, but he remembered the way. He began to notice the familiar scents that he associated with the old fishing hole and started hearing the water running from the spillway.

Tom eased his truck across the dam, paying more attention to the fish that were striking across the pond than the narrow road in front of him.

Unable to hide his enthusiasm, Rex ran from the front of the truck back to the tailgate, throwing his head back with each bark. There was no doubt that the young Lab was excited to see the pond. At that moment, Tom knew he was seeing the dog Rex had been before the surgery.

"Okay, boy, hold your horses," he said, walking to the back of the truck. As soon as the leash was hooked to Rex's collar, the tailgate opened, and the young Lab jumped to the ground and made a beeline to the pond, then dove front-feet-first into the water.

"Well, that answers that question," Tom said as he stood holding the other end of the leash and watching Rex swim parallel to the dam.

For the next several minutes, Rex swam like there was never any doubt of it. Occasionally he stepped out of the water, shook himself off, and dove back in.

"I knew a three-legged dog could swim, but now I know my three-legged dog can swim," Tom joked as he watched his dog play.

Reaching inside his truck, Tom pulled out the old, dingy, yellow duck that Rex loved so much. He knew his Lab had only passed the first part of the test for that day. The second part would be the hardest part, but also the most important one.

It didn't take long for the Lab to notice the duck in Tom's hand. Once he saw the toy, the young dog sat still in the water, waiting to see what would happen next.

Tom tossed the duck toward Rex, and it landed a few feet short of where he sat. The three-legged dog wasted no time grabbing the toy out of the water with his mouth and climbing onto the bank with it.

Carrying the stuffed duck, Rex followed Tom onto the pier. They walked to the very end of the wooden structure and sat down. This wasn't the first time the two of them found themselves sitting together at the end of that old pier, but ordinarily, it would be after Rex wore himself out fetching the old dingy duck, not before.

There was a reason why Tom had hooked the leash to Rex before he let him off the bed of the truck. It was a safety precaution. If the young, three-legged Lab found himself in trouble while swimming, Tom could have pulled back on the strap and helped his dog make it back to dry land.

Even though Rex needed no help for the first water test, Tom was still concerned. He knew that swimming back and forth along the bank was one thing, but jumping off the pier into the deep part of the pond was another. He also realized that he would have to take the leash off his dog for him to make the first jump off the pier.

"You ready, boy?" Tom asked. He sat there scratching up and down Rex's back while the dog stared out across the pond, holding the stuffed duck in his mouth.

After a few minutes, Tom stood. "Come on, boy. We got this." He tugged on the strap as he walked to the front of the pier.

Rex followed, still holding the duck, wagging his nub because he knew what was about to take place.

At the beginning of the pier, Tom kneeled and unhooked the leash from his dog's collar. He used both hands and rubbed the young Lab's head and neck. "Don't make me jump in after you. It's been many years since I've dived into this pond, and I'd like it to stay that way."

Rex dropped the duck on the ground and nudged Tom's hand to encourage him to pick it up. He then trotted toward the end of the pier, seemly unbothered by the fact that he was missing one of his hind legs. The young dog seemed happy to be on that wooden dock and anxious for his favorite toy to be thrown.

Tom snatched the duck from his feet. "Okay, boy, here goes," he said, tossing the toy parallel with the pier over Rex's head and toward the middle of the pond.

Watching the stuffed animal fly through the air, Rex dug his front claws into the wood for traction. He began to run on the wooden planks toward the middle of the pond.

"Run, boy!" Tom yelled as he started walking behind his fetching partner.

Tom could see Rex gaining speed with every stride as he heard his own feet pound the wood of the dock. As he watched his dog get closer to the water, there came a moment when Tom recognized that there was no turning back for Rex. The three-legged Lab was going into the water, whether it was by jumping or by falling. Tom yelled again for Rex to run, hoping the encouragement would make a difference.

Rex saw precisely where the yellow duck had landed in the pond. He ran as if he carried no doubt that he would jump and land directly on top of the stuffed animal just like countless times before.

Reaching the end of the pier, he readied himself for the takeoff like always, eyeing his target and saving an extra burst of speed for just before he pushed off with his front legs, but this time was different. This time his final push would come from one hind leg, not two.

Tom continued to walk toward the end of the pier, becoming more concerned with each step. He knew Rex wasn't running fast enough to make the distance he needed to reach the duck.

Not only was the young Lab slower than usual, but his stride was clumsy also. Tom quickly started questioning whether having Rex try the jump was a good idea.

The Lab started the jump cleanly, using all the strength he could muster to launch his body away from the pier with his two front legs.

When it came time to use his back leg, the difference was obvious. The instant bounce from the dock that Tom ordinarily would see was not there. The determined Lab only achieved half the distance he needed to reach the duck, landing awkwardly in the water on his side.

The landing sounded like a piece of plywood hitting flush with the pond.

"Well, that sounded as bad as it looked," Tom said to himself.

By now he was standing at the jump-off point, never losing sight of his dog as Rex righted himself in the water to swim toward the yellow duck.

Since the jump covered less distance, that meant the young Lab would have farther to swim.

"Come on, boy," Tom whispered as he watched his three-legged dog struggle to finish what he had started.

The stuffed duck drifted farther away from the pier and began to sink as it absorbed the pond water. Finally reaching his prize, Rex scooped the toy in his mouth and made the turn to head back to the bank.

Tom stood and watched as his dog swam closer, lifting the toy up above the water line as if he was trying to keep it from drowning. The closer the Lab got to land, the better Tom felt.

Slowly but steadily, the young Lab made it back to the bank, shaking himself off as he stepped out of the water. He met Tom at the pier and dropped the stuffed animal on the ground so it could be thrown once more.

It became apparent that getting the duck back on dry land had taken more out of Rex than usual.

"Oh no, not doing that again today. We need to strengthen that back leg of yours before we throw anything that far out in the pond again. That landing of yours could use some work also."

Even though getting it was somewhat painful, Tom had his answer about the Jumpathon. Though it wasn't pretty at times, Rex proved swimming wasn't a problem for him, and jumping off the dock into the water bothered Tom more than it bothered his three-legged Lab.

He allowed Rex to swim along the bank a few more minutes before he loaded him onto the back of the truck. "I can't wait to see the look on Ms. Cash's face," he said as he shut the tailgate.

13

STRONGER
AND FASTER

Rex sat on the edge of the grass, dripping wet, watching every move his master made.

Tom stood halfway between the three-legged Lab and the jump-off point of the ramp, holding the stuffed duck down by his side.

Two months had passed since Rex's first jump into the pond after his surgery—two months filled with running, diving and swimming.

Tom made Rex's training for the Jumpathon a hobby, with the black Lab loving every minute of it. The three-legged dog enjoyed everything about practicing, and he loved to jump off that pier. Plus, the extra time he got to spend with his favorite human made it even better.

Once Rex was strong enough, Tom began taking him to the city park, where the public ramp was set up so local dogs could practice for the competition. This was also where the Jumpathon would be held, so he wanted his dog to become comfortable jumping off that particular ramp.

"You ready, boy?"

Hearing the question, Rex eased up into a standing position at the start of the ramp, never taking his eyes off the yellow duck in Tom's hand.

"Go!" Tom yelled as he slung the stuffed toy up in the air toward the water.

Smoothly with no wasted motion, the three-legged Lab ran down the ramp, using every inch of it before he leaped toward his toy that hadn't even hit the water yet.

"My goodness, that was a nice jump," Tom said to himself. As he stood there watching Rex swim toward his toy, he heard clapping behind him. He turned and saw it was Hope.

"Yep, snuck up on ya, didn't I? Now, what if I would have just kept walking and pushed you into the water? I wonder if Rex would have tried to save you. Can you imagine? Jumping in the water because of a duck and coming out with a wet turkey."

Tom smiled and shook his head. "First of all, that would have been uncalled for and mean. Second of all, you are assuming that I would have needed saving. And yes, I do believe Rex would have saved me."

Hope couldn't help but laugh out loud.

Tom looked up at the sky. "So, what, you came all the way down here just to make fun of me?"

"Well, that was part of the reason. The other part was to see how the training is going."

"It's going well. Remembering Rex two months ago and looking at him now, he's like a different dog. All of his confidence is back. He's more playful than he was back then, and his back leg is stronger. He jumps around on that leg like a kid on a pogo stick.

"When I first started letting him jump after the surgery, I just wanted him to be able to compete, but now, I don't know, he may have a chance at winning the local contest."

"Really?" Hope asked.

"Yeah, I mean, I've been to a couple of these Jumpathons, so I remember how far the local dogs were jumping. Most of the dogs are entered just for fun. Some of them will be walking on this ramp for the first time that day. Rex should be one of the three or four dogs that have a legitimate chance to win."

By this time, Tom's wet Lab had made it back onto dry land, nudging Hope's hand with the yellow duck in his mouth.

"I believe he's trying to tell you something," Tom said. Hope squatted with her knees.

"Bless his heart, he still has the mark on his nose from the snake bite." She noticed the scar as she rubbed his head and ears.

The young dog stood there and enjoyed the attention for a few seconds but then dropped the duck in front of Hope, sounding off a playful bark and wagging his nub.

Hope picked up the stuffed toy and walked toward the end of the ramp with the black Lab eyeballing her the whole time.

She stopped. "You ready, Rex?"

Rex, not moving a muscle, continued to stare at the duck.

"Go get it," she yelled, tossing the toy toward the middle of the pond.

This time the black Lab was running before the duck left Hope's hand. With long strides, he made his way toward the water, timing his jump perfectly to plant his back foot at the exact edge of the ramp before using it to push off. The young Lab flew through the air toward the center of the pond, looking as if he was posing for a picture—landing front-feet-first just inches from the stuffed duck.

"Holy crap, that may be the farthest I've ever seen him jump," Tom said, sounding surprised.

"You're welcome," Hope replied.

"Hope, if he starts jumping like that, not only will he win the local competition on day one, but he might also be able to outlast a few of those professional dogs the next day. I can't wait to see the look on Ms. Cash's face."

"Slow down, Mr. Jumpathon. Remember what your goal was two months ago. You just wanted him to be able to jump with the other dogs. Be careful not to get your hopes too high. Rex is already a winner, because he has survived everything that's been thrown at him during his young life."

"I guess you have a point," Tom agreed.

"You guess? Think about it; he's taken from his momma early because some big cat attacks their dog pen. He then picks a fight with a log skidder trying to save a puppy. And we're not even sure what happened to the poor thing the night he broke his leg. Then he saves Lucky from getting bitten by a snake."

"Hearing you say all that, I'm starting to think he's bad luck," Tom added.

Hope gave him one of those looks he hated so much and continued, "To top it all off, having you for an owner can't be easy. The poor fellow has scars all over his body, and he is still just as loving as he was as a puppy."

Tom walked up to Hope and put his arm around her.

"Everything you just said is true. And I'm happy that Rex is acting like the dog I knew before the leg amputation, but I guess seeing him make a jump like that gets me excited. I hope the three of us have fun that day, no matter how Rex finishes in the competition."

"I agree, but can I give you some advice?" Hope asked.

"Could I stop you?" Tom replied.

Ignoring the question, she called Rex out of the water and back onto the ramp.

"I watched you guys from my car for a while before I walked down here. I noticed that every time you threw the duck, it seemed as if Rex was looking for it as he ran. So, I believe if the duck leaves his line of sight, it distracts him."

"So, you think I'm throwing the toy too high, therefore slowing him down?"

"Well, actually, you just said it," Hope answered.

Tom thought for a moment. "You know, that makes sense. That dog is concentrating on the duck so hard before I throw it that if he loses sight of it while it's in the air, it becomes a distraction."

Tom wanted to do one more jump to test Hope's theory before they left the park. Again, Rex outdid himself, landing in the water well past his usual distance.

"It's getting dark; we better call it a day," Tom said as he watched Rex swim back to the bank one last time.

"So, when is the Jumpathon?" Hope asked.

"It starts two weeks from today."

"Well, I think he's ready. You may even want to ease up on the training. You don't want to burn him out on it," Hope suggested.

Tom loaded Rex onto the back of the truck. "Yeah, I need to keep him excited about jumping, so a couple days off might help. Make him miss it a little."

▲ ▲ ▲

Hope blew a piece of hair out of her face as she stood in the middle of the room and admired her work. "Another room painted—this is cause for a celebration," she mumbled to herself, thinking about the gallon of chocolate ice cream inside her icebox.

Slowly but surely, she was finishing the renovation of the upstairs part of her house. Every time she checked off something from her to-do list, she felt more confident about her decision to buy that old place.

Before she could make it downstairs to her ice cream, the phone rang. It was Tom.

"Hello," she answered.

"Let me guess; you're putting up drywall."

"Nope."

"Okay, I bet you are installing light fixtures," he suggested.

"You would lose that bet. Actually, I just finished painting one of the upstairs bedrooms, and I'm heading to the kitchen to claim my reward."

"Ice cream," Tom said, laughing.

The conversation continued as Hope walked into the kitchen and opened the door to the icebox.

"I found out some bad news today, and I need to ask a favor."

Hope quickly noticed the change in Tom's tone, becoming more serious. "Okay, what's the matter?"

"I found out today that I've got to fly to Memphis tomorrow for work and I won't be back until Friday afternoon. The terminal up there has a flu epidemic, and people are calling in sick left and right. It has gotten so bad that the company is flying people in from other terminals to help out. My flight leaves tomorrow morning from Mobile at six o'clock. The plan is to have me at the Memphis terminal working by nine in the morning."

"Okay, so you need a dog sitter for Rex and Lucky. No problem," Hope volunteered as she dropped a scoop of ice cream into a bowl.

"Well I do need a dog sitter, but I also want you to do something else for me. The Jumpathon starts Friday morning, so I need you to take Rex and stand in for me," he explained.

Hope wasn't quick to answer.

"You still there?" Tom asked.

"You realize that tomorrow is Tuesday?"

"I do."

"That doesn't leave us much time to work together. Tom, I don't know, I'm not sure if Rex will jump for me."

"What?" Tom asked. "Sure he will; he loves you. Besides, one of the longest jumps I ever saw him make was when you threw for him."

Hope's ice cream melted while she stood there, trying to find a way to get out of helping Tom without letting him and Rex down. "What about Mike? Have you asked him?"

"I thought about him, but you know I can't count on Mike for something like this. He might show up; then again he may not."

Hope would have loved to argue with Tom about Mike, but she knew what he said was true. "What about Fred?"

Tom explained to Hope that Fred's wife was having surgery that Thursday.

"Tom, you know I hate to be in front of crowds. There could easily be three hundred people there to watch those dogs jump."

Tom wasn't going to tell Hope, but according to Dr. Wright, the Oakville Humane Society had already sold over four hundred tickets for the event.

"Hope, you will do fine. Heck, most of the time, Rex minds you better than me anyway. He may even jump farther with you there."

"You're just trying to get back at Ms. Cash," Hope said.

Tom couldn't deny that was some of his motivation. "Do you believe she had the nerve to call me last night and again try to talk me out of entering Rex? I can't lie: that's part of it, but not all of it. I just hate the idea of him not being able to show everybody how well he can jump. We have put a lot of work into getting ready for it."

"You are killing me," Hope complained.

"So, you will do it?"

"I guess I don't have a choice. I'm not going to let Ms. Cash win."

"Yes! Thank you. If I were there I'd give you a big, wet, sloppy kiss," Tom said.

"If you were here, I'd punch you in the face," Hope admitted.

14

MORE MOTIVATION

Vito relaxed on the back of the couch in Hope's living room and watched the front door swing open, allowing the sunlight to escape inside the house along with Lucky and Rex.

Quiet and calm, the black and white cat stayed on his perch and waited as the two dogs walked around and made themselves at home.

Hope was somewhat confident that all three animals could coexist under the same roof for a few days, so she decided not to take Vito to her sisters. Hope's doubt was not about her cat's safety but the two visitors' wellbeing.

"No slapping, Vito," she yelled as she dropped her car keys on the coffee table.

Rex walked to his favorite spot in front of the fireplace, carrying his yellow duck in his mouth and seemingly not noticing the cat watching him.

Lucky, on the other hand, immediately found Vito's location and didn't mind acting concerned. The old dog knew the cat well enough to be mindful of where it was and keep his distance.

Hope pulled two treats from her jeans pocket and dropped one at Lucky's front feet. "You know I'm buttering you up for something, don't you, old man?" she asked as Lucky chewed on the treat.

She bent down and gently grabbed the old dog to take him upstairs. The Jumpathon started the next day, but all the local dogs had to be at the park by two o'clock the day before to register and to pass a swim test.

"This may not be necessary, but I wouldn't feel right leaving you and Vito here alone without separating you guys," she explained as she carried Lucky and his water bowl upstairs.

"This may save you from getting another scar on your nose."

Lucky sat by his water and watched as Hope closed the bedroom door behind her.

Once the door closed, she heard Rex let out a bark. Jogging down the staircase, Hope saw the black and white cat standing about three feet from the young Lab, luring him within striking distance.

"Vito, get back on that couch!" She picked up her pace down the stairs. The cat quickly ran back to its perch.

"Okay, pretty boy, you ready to go show everyone how good a swimmer you are?"

Rex stood, wagged his nub and grabbed the stuffed duck off the floor with his mouth as the leash fell around his neck.

The large cat commented with a sharp meow, disapproving of the attention that the young Lab received.

"What's wrong, Vito? Are you jealous?" Hope asked as she led Rex to the front door.

▲ ▲ ▲

Rex hung his head out of the backseat window as the car slowly came to a stop at the park.

"My gosh, the people," Hope whispered.

The three-legged Lab let out a bark of approval once he realized where he and Hope were.

"There must be thirty dogs here."

There were closer to forty dogs there, along with all the dog owners and all the local Humane Society board members. The local newspaper had also sent a reporter. Since there was potential for a photo op, the mayor was there, along with the police chief and fire chief.

There were also two groups of elementary school students on class field trips to watch the dogs swim.

"My god at all these people, we're not even jumping today. I'm going to kill Tom for this, perform CPR on him, then kill him again," Hope said.

She approached the crowd, carrying the stuffed duck with one hand and holding Rex's leash with the other.

The second Dr. Wright saw Hope and the bobtailed Lab, he smiled and motioned for them to come to the judge's table.

"There you are," the old doctor yelled. "I was beginning to get worried that we would lose a jumper."

"No, sir," Hope answered. "Tom had to go out of town for work, so I'm taking his place with Rex. Just tell me where to sign and what to do."

Ms. Cash stood close enough to the judge's table to hear the conversation between Hope and Dr. Wright. "Good afternoon," she announced as she walked toward the table.

"Hello," Hope answered, trying her best to be polite.

"Dr. Wright, I hate to interrupt, but isn't there a rule that says a dog's owner must be present during registration?" Ms. Cash asked.

Hearing the question, Hope looked up at the old doctor but never stopped filling out the paperwork.

"No, Ms. Cash, to my knowledge, there is no such rule," Dr. Wright replied.

"I'm sure there has to be," Ms. Cash continued.

The old doctor smiled, shook his head then reached under the judge's table and pulled a half-inch-thick booklet from a book bag.

"Here you are," he said. He handed the reading material to Ms. Cash.

"What is this?"

"That's the Jumpathon rulebook. If you find anything in there that says the owner must be present during registration, I want you to let me know. In fact, I'm kind of curious about that myself since you brought it up."

Hope never said a word as she continued to fill out the paperwork before her. "I think that does it," she said as she signed the last form.

The gray-haired doctor carefully looked over each page. "Okay, you and Rex follow me," he said.

He cleared a path through the crowd as they walked toward the lake. Hope couldn't help but wonder about the conversation she had just heard.

"Dr. Wright, wait a minute, what happens if Ms. Cash finds what she's looking for in the rulebook?"

The old doctor stopped and turned to look at Hope.

"I wouldn't worry about Ms. Cash finding anything in that silly rulebook."

"How can you be so sure?" Hope asked.

"Because I'm the person who wrote it. I just wanted to keep her busy while we get this swim test out of the way. With any luck, you and Rex will be back home before she gives up looking."

As they walked toward the lake, a crowd began to form behind them and follow.

"What are they doing?" Hope asked.

"I guess they want to see if this three-legged dog can swim," the old doctor answered.

Standing at the water's edge, Dr. Wright explained what he needed to see for the test.

"Okay, Hope, you see the orange post out there sticking out above the water? All I need is for Rex to swim out to that post and back. I will need him to do it twice to make sure he's okay in the water. Now, that post is precisely twenty-five feet away. I'm asking you just like I've asked everyone who came before you. Are you confident he can do it?"

"I'm sure. He may be slower than the other dogs, but he can do it," she answered.

As more people gathered to watch, the crowd's noise became louder. Laughter escaped from different groups within the crowd.

Hope unhooked the leash from the young Lab's collar. "Okay, Rex, this shouldn't be a problem. Let's get this over with before the whole town ends up here."

Off his leash, the black Lab walked chest-deep into the lake, then he turned to face Hope and barked.

Hope held the yellow duck out from her body to get Rex's attention. Ignoring all the people and all the noise, the young dog stood, ears perked, focused and waiting for the duck to fly.

"Go get it!" Hope yelled as she threw the duck up in the air past the top of the orange post.

The three-legged dog instantly dove in after the duck, swimming as fast as he could toward his prize. The crowd began to clap as Rex reached the yellow duck and grabbed it before he turned to make his way back to Hope. The laughter heard earlier was not as widespread as before but was louder, originating from one group of guys in the back.

"Okay, once more," Dr. Wright instructed as Rex walked out of the lake and nudged the old man's knee with the stuffed animal.

"I think he wants you to throw it," Hope said.

Dr. Wright reluctantly took the duck from the young dog's mouth and tossed it toward the post.

One of the larger guys from the group supplying the laughter in the crowd yelled something as the black Lab once again swam toward the floating duck.

"Hey, how long is this going to take?"

Unable to make out the guy's words over the crowd's applause, Hope ignored him as she watched Rex save his toy.

Unsatisfied with the lack of response, the young man yelled again, this time louder. "I didn't know there would be a sick, lame, and lazy division tomorrow."

The group around the young man erupted with cheers, encouraging him to say more.

Hope heard him loud and clear that time.

The black Lab, unaware of the cruel humor, continued to swim slowly toward Hope, doing his best to keep his stuffed duck above the water.

"Easy, Hope," Dr. Wright said.

A few seconds of silence passed before the heckler yelled again. "Hey, lady, I got a good name for your dog. You could call him Tripod!"

By now Hope's face was firetruck red. "Who is that?" she asked Dr. Wright.

"That is Ms. Cash's nephew."

"What's his name?" she asked.

"His name is Paul, but it's best—"

Before Dr. Wright could finish his sentence, Hope hung Rex's leash around his neck.

"If this goes badly, take Rex home with you," she instructed.

"Young lady, come back here," the old doctor begged.

Paul, who wasn't from Oakville, was in his early twenties and had an athletic build. He did not know that the lady walking toward him had competed on the boy's wrestling team in high school and had been a junior college All-American female wrestler just five years before.

Any anxiety she felt about being in front of all those people quickly turned into anger. Sure, she didn't enjoy crowds, but she disliked mean-spirited people more, and she hated bullies with a pink and purple passion.

Hope halved the distance between her and Paul.

"What's wrong, lady, did I hurt your feelings?" he yelled. He then noticed that two of his buddies had disappeared into the crowd.

Hope pulled a rubber band from her back pocket and tied her hair into a short ponytail.

"What are you doing?" Paul asked.

"Oh, I just thought since you had so much to say that I would get closer so I could hear you better. You must think you are a funny guy?"

Every eye in the crowd was on Hope. Paul looked around once more to find he was no longer in a group of people but was standing alone.

"Look, lady, I was just having some fun. I don't care if your dog jumps tomorrow or not."

Hope took a piece of gum from her mouth and dropped it onto the ground. She talked in a voice loud enough for the whole crowd to hear.

"You wanna know what I think, Paul?" Hope asked. "I think up until today, no one has ever stood up to you. I also believe you are a bully who loves attention. Something happened to you somewhere down the line to cause you to act this way. What happened to you, Paul? Were you bullied as a kid?"

The young man looked around to see everyone staring at him. Having craved attention from the crowd a few minutes earlier, he now found himself wanting to distance himself from that same group. "Okay, whatever, this whole dog jumping business is hokey anyway. I'm out of here." He turned to walk away.

Hope felt a hand on her shoulder as she watched Paul vanish into the crowd. It was Dr. Wright, who had made sure her partner was back on his leash. She felt Rex's cold, wet nose touch the side of her hand.

"Sweet boy," she said as she kneeled and rubbed his head and ears. "What's wrong with people like that?"

"You handled that pretty well," Dr. Wright answered.

"Yeah, I guess so. I was kind of hoping I would at least get to put him in a headlock," she replied with a smile.

▲ ▲ ▲

Standing in Hope's lap, Vito seemed very unamused by the two house guests lying on the living room floor.

"Life is hard sometimes, isn't it?" Hope said as she massaged the fat cat's back.

The peaceful silence ended when the phone rang.

"Hello," Hope answered.

"Girl, what did you do today?" Tom asked from the other end of the line.

"What on earth are you talking about?" Hope already knew the answer.

"I heard you were about to throw down with some guy over Rex. I had four voicemails waiting for me when I got off."

Hope explained what had happened earlier that day. "Look, you know I can't stand to see someone bullied. Plus, poor Rex couldn't defend himself. If the guy hadn't said the word 'tripod,' I would have let it go."

Tom told Hope that one of the voicemails was from Mike, who said the newspaper reporter who was there planned to do a story about her. "You and Rex are going to be local celebrities."

"Well, so much for not wanting a lot of attention," Hope joked.

15

THE WORD GETS OUT

Tom walked into the hotel dining area, pulling his suitcase behind him, and placed his backpack on the first table he reached. It was the third and final day that he would endure the hotel's free breakfast. While 'free' doesn't always mean 'inadequate,' it did in this case. He hadn't eaten anything from that kitchen worth trying a second time.

As he stood there deciding between the waffle maker or the sausage, eggs, and grits in the mini buffet, he noticed a morning Memphis newspaper that someone had left on the table beside his. He looked around, but no one was there to claim it, so he slowly pulled it over and placed it under his backpack.

"Well, I haven't tried the waffles yet," he said to himself. A few minutes later, he sat at his table with a plate full of waffles drowned in syrup and two small cartons of milk.

Chewing his first bite, he placed the backpack on the floor and opened the newspaper. Tom always read the sports section first, and this morning was no different.

Nothing on the front page of the sports that day looked interesting enough to make Tom read past the headlines. Cramming the second bite into his mouth with a fork, he turned the page, and a picture on page three immediately caught his attention. The photo showed a dog swimming with a stuffed duck in its mouth.

"Huh, that dog has a duck, just like Rex," he mumbled, still chewing.

By now, the dining area had begun to get crowded as the hotel guests started their day. Tom continued looking at the picture and realized that the dog in the photo was also a black Lab. He then noticed something that almost made him choke on his breakfast. The dog in the paper was not only a black Lab but also bobtailed.

"Holy hambone." He reached for his milk to wash his food down.

Before he could take a swallow, he noticed a second picture at the bottom of the page. This one made him push the plate of waffles away, giving the newspaper his full attention.

"That's Hope!" he yelled.

Everybody in the kitchen and dining room stopped to look in Tom's direction.

"Sorry, folks, I just saw a picture of my girlfriend from back home in this newspaper. I was not expecting that this morning."

Tom finally read the caption at the bottom of the first picture. "Three-legged bobtailed black Lab from Alabama jumps for the trophy."

He took another bite of waffle and laughed. "He's not jumping for a trophy; he's jumping because we keep throwing his duck in the water."

Tom's first impulse was to call Hope and tell her what he had found. But the more he thought about it, the more he felt it wouldn't be a good idea. He knew Hope was already uncomfortable with the attention she was getting locally. How would she feel if she knew her picture was in a Memphis newspaper?

▲ ▲ ▲

Sobriety was a habit that Victor Evans had given up on years ago, but if you wanted to find him sober, the best time was during the annual Jumpathon.

Since the first one had been partially his idea, the local Humane Society Board allowed him to be a judge every year with the stipulation that he remain sober during the competition.

Wearing his best seersucker suit, Mr. Evans walked amongst the crowd in the park that morning, shaking hands and making small talk with people as if he was running for mayor again.

"Good morning, Ms. Cash, you are looking extra nice today," Victor said as they walked toward the judges' table.

"Mr. Evans, have you been drinking?" she asked in a very judgmental tone.

"Well, Ms. Cash, that's sad that you think I would have to be drunk to believe that you look extra nice," he answered with a chuckle.

"What? No. What do you want, Victor? I'm busy at the moment."

"I just thought you would want to know: there's a TV reporter from Montgomery walking around, asking people questions."

Ms. Cash immediately stopped and gave the old man all her attention. "You are drunk, Victor. You know the agreement you have with the board. You cannot be drinking during the Jumpathon if you want to continue to be a judge."

Victor looked down at the ground with disappointment and shook his head.

"Ms. Cash, I assure you I have not had a drink in the past thirty-six hours. Look, see that van parked by the park entrance? That's a TV truck, and there is a cameraman inside that van. I just spent the last fifteen minutes talking to a delightful reporter."

Ms. Cash looked at the van and turned back to Victor. "Okay, so why are they here? We've never had a television station cover this event before."

Victor pulled a half-smoked cigarette from his pants pocket and put it in his mouth.

"They've come to see Rex," he said as he reached for his lighter.

Ms. Cash thought for a second. "Rex? Rex who?" she said again in the judgmental tone but now with a look of confusion.

"It's not Rex who, it's Rex the dog, Tom's black Lab that's jumping today."

Ms. Cash's look of confusion quickly turned to anger. "You mean the three-legged dog?" she asked harshly.

"That's the one. That reporter said they were here to do a story that would air on her station's six o'clock newscast tonight."

Mr. Evans noticed that Ms. Cash had become very quiet, which was highly unusual. Her idea that having a three-legged dog in the Jumpathon would only bring ridicule to the town's image was as strong as ever.

"Are you okay?" he asked.

"No, Victor, I'm not okay. But I'm about to let my feelings be known." She turned and walked off.

Dr. Wright sat at the judges' table, writing a checklist of tasks to complete before the first dog jumped. The old doctor had arrived at the park that morning just before sun-up. He was glad the first day of the Jumpathon had finally arrived but would be even happier when it was over. "I'm getting too old and slow for this," he mumbled to himself.

As he sat there going over his notes, Dr. Wright heard something slam onto the judges' table. It was the copy of the rulebook he had given Ms. Cash yesterday.

"Good morning," he said without even looking up.

"I'm very disappointed in you, Dr. Wright," she said, her tone judgmental.

"I can't imagine why."

"Not only did you send me on a fishing expedition for something that wasn't there, but you also did it on purpose. I was halfway through that rulebook when I remembered who wrote it," the angry lady explained.

Dr. Wright took off his reading glasses and stuck them in his shirt pocket. "Ms. Cash, yesterday you asked me a question about the rules of this competition, and I gave you an honest answer. You didn't believe me, so I gave you the rulebook so you could look for yourself. Now if you will excuse me, I have more things to do than I have time to do them."

Ms. Cash placed both hands on her hips. "It's just a shame that that three-legged dog will be allowed in this competition. And to make matters worse, a TV crew is here from Montgomery to do a story about him. Our community will be the punchline for other towns across the state."

Not needing to hear any more, Dr. Wright stood up from his chair and turned to leave. After three steps, he stopped and turned back around.

"Ms. Cash, did you see Rex do his swim test yesterday?"

"No, I did not," she answered rudely.

"Well, I did, and I saw something I have never seen before. I saw almost everybody here stop what they were doing and follow that dog down to the lake to watch him swim. Not only did they follow him, but they also cheered and clapped for him during his test. Now, I'm not sure why that happened, but I know this town needs more of that. I also feel like those people here yesterday cheering for Rex will be back again today to buy a ticket to watch him jump. That's why I still do this every year. Moments like yesterday when dogs and people connect don't happen often, but they do happen."

"Are you done, Dr. Wright?" Ms. Cash asked.

"Just one more thing: I've known Rex since he was a puppy. He's a smart, well-mannered, beautiful dog with a lot of gumption. Animals like that, even if it's only for a short time, have a way of making us humans forget about ourselves and our problems. You think a three-legged dog being in our contest will somehow hurt our town. Well, I think just the opposite. I believe his jumping today could help some people. And at the very least, it will bring a smile to some faces. What matters is that people see him out here trying to do something he truly loves even though his odds of winning are not good. We all could learn a lesson from that, Ms. Cash."

The lady, who just a few seconds before had stood before Dr. Wright with her hands on her hips and a sour look, now looked disheartened. "Maybe I've been looking at this all wrong. I guess I didn't think this through; I was more concerned about the town's image than about the people in the town," she said, sounding almost embarrassed.

"Ms. Cash, being wrong happens to the best of us sometimes. Now, if you will excuse me, I've got more on my plate than I can pray over right now."

16

THE BIG DAY

Hope and Rex sat on a blanket atop a hill overlooking the lake at the park. From there they watched the crowd grow as car after car pulled through the entrance.

Sleep had not been kind to Hope the night before. She hadn't experienced this much anxiety since she wrestled in college. She felt her heartbeat accelerate as she watched more people drive into the park. The palms of her hands began to sweat as the Jumpathon start time approached.

"I almost forgot how this felt," she said to herself.

Rex fetched the yellow duck and dropped it in her lap.

"Why am I stressed out? You are doing all the work today, not me," she whispered to Rex as she massaged his ears.

The three-legged Lab quickly leaned in and stole a kiss from Hope's chin while he wagged his nub as if to say "Hey, look at me." He then sat directly in front of her and tilted his head to one side as if to ask her how she was feeling. Hope began to focus on the black Lab as he looked back at her. Throughout the next couple of minutes, her heartbeat gradually returned to normal as she rubbed his head and neck.

After a few more minutes of silence, Hope felt like herself again. As she stood to throw the duck once more, her cell phone rang. It was Tom.

"Hello," she answered.

"Just checking on you guys before he makes his first jump. I'm about to board the plane."

"I'm just sitting here having a panic attack. Other than that, everything is great."

"You okay?" Tom asked.

"Yeah, actually, Rex helped calm me down. You have a very relaxing dog here."

"Hope, I know this isn't easy for you, so if you need to back out, I understand. I mean, let's be honest: Rex wouldn't even know the difference."

"Oh no, we are doing this. That's not the first panic attack I've been through; I'll be okay. You get home so we can fight over who gets to keep this ribbon he and I are about to win."

With the high in the low seventies, it felt like room temperature that day at the Oakville City Park. The sun shined bright, the sky was blue, and the wind was calm.

"Folks, we couldn't have ordered better weather for today," the announcer yelled over the PA system.

The dog handlers were told to have their dogs at the jump ramp at nine o'clock sharp that morning to decide the day's jumping order. Each owner stood side by side with their dog in front while a judge passed around a plastic bucket of numbers. One by one, the owners picked a piece of paper from the container that would decide when each dog would jump.

Hope, the third person to pick, pulled number fifteen. She wasn't sure how to feel about being last, but she was happy she and Rex wouldn't have to jump first.

Once the drawing finished, the announcer stated that dog number one would need to be on the ramp within ten minutes. Each dog had to complete two jumps and would have seven minutes after the first jump to swim out of the water, make it back onto the ramp, and finish the second jump. Once a dog finished their second jump, the next dog would have three minutes to be ready on the ramp for their first attempt.

Two judges at the judges' table kept time between jumps, while two judges in two boats on the lake measured the length of the jumps.

"Rex, the best is going to be saved for last today, which means we have some time to kill," Hope said as she looked around at the crowd.

Standing there wondering about ways to pass the time, she noticed Rex was looking toward the judges' table. He let out a bark.

"Whatcha see, boy?" she asked.

He stood and began pulling her toward the judges.

"Where are you going? We can't bother Dr. Wright; he's busy."

Hope didn't know that even though Rex loved Dr. Wright, the old doctor was not the reason she was being pulled toward that table. She had no way of knowing the history Rex and Victor Evans shared.

At the judges' table, Rex sat down directly across from Victor and barked loudly. The barks eventually turned into growls as he watched the ex-mayor. Victor knew why this was happening, but he wasn't going to try to explain the reason today. With only a cheap folding table and a large cup of hot coffee between him and the angry dog, Victor became uneasy.

"Hope, please control your dog," he ordered.

"I'm sorry, Mr. Evans, I don't know why he's doing this. He doesn't normally treat strangers this way."

"Okay, he seems pretty aggressive. How about moving him along?"

Hope agreed that putting distance between Rex and Victor was a good idea, so she tightened the Lab's leash to lead him away. As he stood, the upset Lab used his snout to pick up his end of the table, causing the cup of coffee to tilt and spill into Mr. Evans' lap.

"Oh my god, that's hot!" Victor yelled. He stood and quickly pulled his soaked pants away from his legs. Rex let out another loud bark.

"No," Hope cried as she grabbed the dog's collar so he couldn't lift the table again. "Mr. Evans, I don't know why he's acting this way, but I'm so sorry. I've never seen him like this toward anybody."

Standing there with a look of disgust and coffee dripping down into his shoes, Mr. Evans knew that Rex owed him that. "Hope, please move along with your dog, or I'll be forced to disqualify him from today's contest."

Holding the leash in one hand and the yellow duck in the other, Hope finally convinced Rex to give up on his revenge and walk toward the concession stand. The smell of cooked food may have also helped persuade the bobtailed Lab.

Two lines of people waited for food.

"We should have time. Let's see if we can find us a snack while we wait for our turn to jump," she reasoned.

Some people smoked when they were nervous; Hope turned to food.

The concession stand was a food truck from Fatbacks. Ms. Pearl loved the Jumpathon because she could park there and sell twice the food with only half the employees compared to her restaurant.

The fifteen dogs competing that day represented a wide range of breeds. There was Red the bloodhound, Dorothy the pit bull, and Bullet the German shepherd. There was Tucker the beagle, Pepper the border collie, and Butters the golden retriever, along with Lola the sooner and Oscar the Rottweiler.

All good dogs, but not all carried the enthusiasm for jumping or swimming that Rex did. A few didn't mind the water but didn't care for the ramp. Some were okay with jumping but didn't enjoy swimming. In two cases, it was even obvious that the owners were more excited to be there than the dogs were.

As they walked and looked for a place to watch the start of the show, Rex grabbed his stuffed duck from Hope's back pocket. He watched as she sat on the bottom row of the bleachers with two hot dogs and a drink. The happy Lab lay down at her feet, resting his head on the yellow duck, content to watch people walk by in front of them.

No sooner could she get her straw into her cup than she felt someone sit beside her.

"You're not going to feed him that hot dog before he jumps, are you?"

"Hey Fred, how's your wife? I heard she had surgery," she asked, trying her best to change the subject.

"Oh, she's fine, it was just her gallbladder. The hospital sent her home yesterday afternoon. She told me to find a place for me and the kids to go today so she could relax. I dropped the boys off on the other side of the park at the baseball fields, so I've got some time to kill. I'm going to wait a couple more hours before I run back and check on her," he said with a smile.

Although she didn't say it aloud, Hope was glad to see Fred. She considered him a friend, and she figured a kind face and friendly conversation would help her relax and pass the time while she waited.

Rex flirted with sleep, only to be startled by the occasional kid walking by asking to pet him. The longer he lay there, the longer the line to see him became. Within a few minutes, that section of bleachers was paying more attention to Rex and his fans than the dogs that were jumping.

"If that dog could hold a pen, I think he would be signing autographs today," Fred commented.

"Yeah, he's soaking up that attention like a sponge," Hope answered.

Fred and Hope sat and talked as the contest started. The first three jumps were uneventful. Each dog seemed happy to be there and did their best. But neither pup could muster an attempt over eight feet. Hope began to think that Rex might be the favorite to win that day.

The bleachers were filling with people sitting elbow-to-elbow.

"Fred, you have been to most of these Jumpathons. Have you ever seen this many people show up?"

"Hope, I don't think I've ever seen this many people gathered in one place at any event in Oakville. People are still buying tickets at the entrance to get in here. From what I hear, some of this is yours and Rex's doing."

"What do you mean?"

"I heard about you standing up to that guy at the swim test yesterday. That's what everybody was talking about at the barbershop this morning. Those guys couldn't wait to see Rex jump today. Then I went to Fatbacks, and all I heard was how a crowd of people followed you and Rex down to the lake for his test."

"What was I supposed to do? I tried to ignore him, but he kept on. The guy had it coming."

"Maybe so, but word has gotten out. You know how news travels around here. I bet a third of these people are here only because of you and that dog."

"So much for helping me relax," she mumbled.

A piercing screech rang through the loudspeakers as the announcer cleared his throat. "Okay, today's next jumper is Tucker the beagle. This is Tucker's first time competing here in Oakville, so let's give him a big welcome."

Most of the people in the crowd were polite enough to clap, but that didn't seem to encourage Tucker. The young beagle had second and maybe third thoughts about walking onto the jump ramp.

Hope enjoyed watching Rex interact with the kids walking by. She felt Fred nudge her with his elbow.

"Watch this little beagle," Fred explained. "He can swim like a fish, but he doesn't like that ramp one bit."

"You can do it, Tucker!" someone shouted from the bleachers, but that did more harm than good because it made the young dog look up and wonder who was calling his name.

Fred was right: Tucker loved to swim, but flying through the air and landing in the water didn't appeal to the little guy.

Just when it looked like Tucker would not be making his appearance on the jump ramp, his owner managed to persuade him not to no-show by pulling some treats from his pocket.

Not to be outsmarted, the young beagle hopped onto the ramp but waited for his treat to drop before he went any farther. Once the encouragement was within reach, he walked toward his reward and grabbed it off the floor of the ramp.

Tucker's handler pulled a tennis ball from another pocket and showed it to his adorable partner. The young beagle started wagging his tail as if he was finally on board with what was about to happen. The handler showed the ball to the crowd, then showed it to Tucker once more before tossing it toward the end of the ramp into the lake.

Once the tennis ball landed in the water, the lovable beagle trotted down to the end of the ramp, stopping at its edge. He turned around to face the crowd, hiked his hind leg up as high he possibly could, and relieved himself right directly in front of the judges. Tucker's handler placed both hands on his head and laughed as the defiant dog baptized the ramp.

"Well, I didn't see that coming," Fred said as he and Hope stood and clapped for the young dog.

"They should give him a trophy," Hope said, almost crying from laughter.

Although Tucker didn't make his jump, he did get the biggest cheer from the crowd that day.

Next came Bullet. "Watch this German shepherd. I think he's going to be the winner today. I've watched most of these dogs jump, and he's the best."

Hope didn't have a comeback to Fred's prediction, so instead she watched as the dog walked onto the ramp.

There was no doubt that Bullet was a full-blooded German shepherd. He had all the physical strengths of the beautiful animal. You could also tell he loved being on that ramp with his handler. The graceful dog efficiently obeyed every command that came his way. And when it was time to jump, he flew off the ramp with speed and purpose.

"That was a nice jump," Hope said.

"Yeah, and his second one will be farther than that. I've watched him a lot while I was out here working with Patch."

The announcer was having a hard time containing his excitement. "Did you see that, folks? That's how you jump into a lake! The judges are measuring the jump as I speak. We should have the distance any—wait, I'm told that Bullet's first jump measured thirteen and a half feet. That's a great jump for the German shepherd!"

The shepherd quickly retrieved the ball from the lake and swam back to dry land. Without any encouragement, Bullet walked back onto the ramp and dropped the ball at his handler's feet.

"Now watch this," Fred whispered as he sat there anticipating the second jump.

Hope began to wonder whom Fred was rooting for, but she wouldn't bother to question him. She was so impressed with the first jump that she didn't dare turn away from the action.

Everyone in the crowd sat mostly in silence and watched as Bullet flew higher and jumped farther the second go-around.

"Told ya," Fred smirked.

"My goodness. Maybe I shouldn't feed Rex this hot dog," Hope admitted.

The announcer yelled over the speakers that Bullet's second jump measured over fifteen feet.

Hope made direct eye contact with the black Lab and started rubbing his ears with both hands. "I've never seen you jump that far, but that doesn't mean you can't do it," she said.

Rex tilted his head and began to hassle. His hassling made it appear that he was smiling back at her.

Fred tapped Hope on the shoulder. "You know, once he gets out there, he's going to be excited, and I've always heard not to eat just before you swim. I'd hate to see him upchuck in front of everybody today, especially since that television reporter is here to do a story on him."

Hope heard Fred's words, but she asked him to repeat it anyway. Once he finished, she knew that hearing it the second time did not make her feel any better.

"I'm not sure if *I* should eat my hot dog now. I might upchuck. Please do me a favor. I need you to find that reporter and if you see her coming my way, stop her. At least keep her away until after Rex jumps."

"How am I supposed to keep her away from you?" he asked.

"I don't know, tell her about Patch. Dig in your wallet and show her some pictures of your kids. Please keep her away from us until after the competition."

"Okay, I'll show her every kid picture I have on me."

While Hope continued to sit and watch the other dogs jump, the crowd around them thinned out. Most of the kids who had made a big deal over Rex eventually found something else to make a big deal over, and Fred was somewhere keeping the TV reporter occupied.

Between the incident with Mr. Evans and finding out that a TV reporter was there to see Rex, it had already been a taxing day for Hope. But then she saw Ms. Cash walking in their direction toward the bleachers.

"I know she's not coming over here to start something," she whispered to herself. The closer Ms. Cash got, the more Hope wanted to grab Rex and run the other way.

"There you guys are. I've been looking all over for you two."

"Look, Ms. Cash, I don't think now is the time to discuss whether Rex should be jumping today," Hope interrupted.

"No, you don't understand. Me and Dr. Wright talked this morning, and he made me realize that I've been wrong about this the whole time, and I'm sorry."

"Really?" Hope asked.

"Yes, I now believe that Rex jumping today is a good thing. I just wanted to meet him and wish you guys all the luck in the world."

Hope's shock made it hard for her to say anything.

"So, this is Rex," Ms. Cash said as she knelt and rubbed the side of his face.

Rex stood to get closer to the friendly lady.

"My goodness, he's wagging that little nub at me," she bragged. She grabbed both sides of the bobtailed Lab's face and started making baby noises at him.

"Careful, Ms. Cash, he likes to give kisses," Hope warned.

"Oh, does he like to steal kisses?" Ms. Cash asked loudly, still using the baby voice.

No sooner had she finished her question than Rex suddenly tilted his head, leaned in, and licked her face from the bottom of her chin to the top of her forehead, almost removing her glasses from her head.

Poor Ms. Cash stood, wiping the dog saliva off while trying not to lose her balance.

"Told ya," Hope reminded her.

"Oh my, I wasn't ready for that," she admitted as she straightened her spectacles.

The stunned busybody pulled a handkerchief from one of her dress pockets and began wiping her forehead with it. Hope could tell she was annoyed.

"Okay, I have a few more people to see. Good luck, you guys. I'm sure you all will do well. Gotta go."

As Hope watched Ms. Cash hurry away, she leaned into Rex.

"Well, we know how to get rid of her from now on, don't we? You should have kissed her sooner."

With only three dogs left before them, Hope decided it would be a good idea to walk Rex down to the water's edge so he could take a quick swim before his time to jump. She thought it would loosen him up and ease her mind off the crowd.

Twenty minutes later, after a few tosses of his duck and a couple of short dives into the lake from the bank, Rex seemed happy to be there and ready to jump.

After his last lap, the wet Lab climbed out of the water, walked to Hope and sat down in front of her with a dead stare.

"I wish I had a camera right now," she said, reaching to take the duck from his mouth.

The three-legged Lab didn't move a muscle as the announcer warned everyone that there was only one dog left to jump that day. The crowd began to cheer and clap because they knew which dog was next.

"That's our cue," Hope whispered to herself. She hooked the leash to Rex's collar and looked into his big, brown eyes. "Okay, sweet boy, let's show 'em what we can do."

17

A STORYTELLER

As Hope closed the book, she looked up to see six sets of eyes peering back at her. Those eyes belonged to six little girls ranging from ages four to seven. Her living room floor was covered with pillows, blankets, and dirty dishes.

"So that's how a bobtailed black Lab found a home, lost a leg, made some friends and became the most popular dog in Oakville," she said. She then stood from the couch to stretch.

"Ms. Hope, can you tell us another story about Rex?" asked a little girl from under one of the blankets. Hope eased back down onto the couch.

"I can, baby girl, but not tonight. It's too late to start another story; I've been reading that book about Rex aloud for the past three hours. I want to see every single one of you get up, brush your teeth, and go to bed."

The youngest of the girls threw her share of a blanket to one side, stood, and tried to rub the sleep out of her eyes. "Mam Me, are those stories in that book true?"

Hope held out both arms toward the sleepy child. "Come here, Joy, before you fall asleep and hurt yourself."

Climbing into Hope's lap, the little girl put her arm around her Mam Me's neck and gave her a big hug.

At this point, all the other kids were waiting on Hope's answer. The house again became quiet and still.

"So, you want to know if those stories are true?"

The young girl brushed her blonde hair out of her face, smiled, and nodded her head.

"Well I can promise you this much: there was a bobtailed three-legged black Lab named Rex, and he may be the smartest and sweetest animal I've ever known. And sometimes it was like that old dog knew what you were thinking. He was also a good friend," she said.

It then became clear to Hope that those girls could ask questions faster than she could answer them.

"Now, ladies, I'm going to say this one more time: I need every one of you to go upstairs and brush your teeth for bed. It's almost midnight, and I'm not going to let you night owls sleep all day tomorrow. We've got work to do in the garden. And by the way, take these blankets and pillows back upstairs as you go, but first I want all these dishes put into the kitchen sink."

A few minutes later, Hope leaned back on the couch and listened to the tiny feet scamper up the stairs. She spent the next few minutes looking up at the ceiling, enjoying the silence. A set of bigger feet came down the stairs. Knowing whose they were, Hope took a deep breath and began to relax.

"Storytime finished?" the young lady asked as she hit the bottom step.

"Katlin, I'm getting too old for this," Hope answered.

"Oh Mom, I'm just now getting you broken in. Besides, you love telling stories about Rex," the young lady said.

Hope placed both hands behind her neck and smiled.

Katlin opened the refrigerator, grabbed a gallon of milk, and set it on the bar. She pulled a loaf of bread and a jar of peanut butter from one of the top cabinets.

"You know, Mom, this is the third slumber party Joy has hosted here, and this is the third time you have kept those kids entertained with that book. That has to be an indication that you have a good story there."

"I've always felt like it was a good story. I just didn't know if I'm a good enough writer to write it."

"Well, I guess I'm biased, but I think you can do anything."

"Thanks, honey."

"Are you nervous about putting something you have written out there for everybody to see?"

"Not really. I was anxious the whole time I was writing it, but once I finished, most of the anxiety went away. I guess I feel like the hard part is over.

"You should have heard your daughter tonight," Hope said, laughing.

"Oh my god, what did she say this time?"

Hope sat up on the edge of the couch. "Nothing terrible. She just asked whether the stories in my book are true."

"Joy loves to hear stories about the three-legged dog, that's for sure," Katlin said.

"Well, so did you when you were her age."

"Yeah, but I didn't have to hear stories. I had the real-life dog licking me in the face every morning. I bet he did that to me every morning for five years. That was his way of getting me out of bed. I still have dreams of him waking me up that way. When I have one of those dreams, I can't help but miss him."

"Rex loved his Katlin," Hope added.

"Okay, Mom, you take the rest of the night off. I'm going to go upstairs and make sure those little troublemakers are not plotting against us and get them in bed. Don't forget to let Coy in for the night."

"Oh my goodness, I started reading to the kids and forgot about Coy being outside."

Hope quickly got up and opened the front door. With no wasted time, Coy trotted in carrying his feed bowl.

"Coy, we just forgot all about you, didn't we?"

The young, black Lab walked straight to the middle of the kitchen, dropped his feed bowl on the floor, and looked up at Hope.

"Well, it doesn't take a dog whisperer to know what you want. Why didn't you bark for us to let you back in, you silly dog?" she said, walking into the kitchen.

Coy let out a loud bark and began to hassle.

"It's too late now," she scolded.

Hope washed the dirty dishes left in the sink while Coy enjoyed his supper.

"Okay, boy, I don't know about you, but I'm ready for bed," she said.

Like every other night, Hope and Coy walked through the house, turning off lights and making sure the doors were locked. Once she was satisfied that everything was how it needed to be, they both headed up the stairs.

At the top of the stairs sat an old trophy case full of awards and trophies. Most had to do with Hope's wrestling days or Katlin's soccer days.

On this night Hope noticed something shiny and red inside the case pushed back in a corner behind two soccer trophies. She opened one of the doors and pulled a slightly dusty ribbon out.

"Good Lord, I forgot this was in here." On the front of the red ribbon were the words "First Round Second Place Oakville Jumpathon 1996."

"Rex, we did good that day. Coy, I think this ribbon deserves better than being pushed back in the corner like that."

Suddenly Hope wasn't as tired as before. With her black Lab following behind her, she walked into the bedroom, opened a closet and pulled out a photo album. She thumbed through the pages and eventually found what she was looking for.

"That's it," she said to herself.

She looked at the three-by-seven photo, then down at her curious Lab, whose ears were perked and head tilted. Coy had no idea what she was doing but didn't mind waiting to find out.

She smiled. "Coy, sometimes you look at me just like your granddaddy would."

With some canned air, she blew most of the dust off the old ribbon and carried it along with the picture she had found back to the trophy case. She pushed back one of her old college wrestling trophies that sat in the center of all the awards.

"I think this is the perfect place for it," she mumbled. She used her trophy as a prop so the red ribbon and picture of Rex holding his yellow duck could lean against it to stand upright.

She gently closed the door of the case. "Okay, Coy, let's go to bed. We've got squash that needs picking and okra that needs cutting in the morning before it gets hot."

While Hope readied herself for sleep, the young, black Lab patrolled the upstairs part of the house, checking each bedroom and making sure everyone was settled.

When he made it into Joy's room, he rested his head on her bed for a minute so he could watch her sleep. Once he was satisfied that his young human was safe, he walked to his pallet at the foot of her bed, picked up his yellow stuffed duck, and like every other night, used it as a pillow.

www.ingramcontent.com/pod-product-compliance
Lightning Source LLC
Chambersburg PA
CBHW061823040426
42447CB00012B/2787